LIVING *the* LUXE LIFE

LIVING *the* LUXE LIFE

The Secrets of Building a Successful Hotel Empire

EFREM HARKHAM
AND MARK BEGO

Skyhorse Publishing

Skyhorse Publishing books may be purchased in bulk at special discounts for sales promotion, corporate gifts, fund-raising, or educational purposes. Special editions can also be created to specifications. For details, contact the Special Sales Department, Skyhorse Publishing, 307 West 36th Street, 11th Floor, New York, NY 10018 or info@skyhorsepublishing.com.

Skyhorse® and Skyhorse Publishing® are registered trademarks of Skyhorse Publishing, Inc.®, a Delaware corporation.

Visit our website at www.skyhorsepublishing.com.

10 9 8 7 6 5 4 3 2 1

Library of Congress Cataloging-in-Publication Data is available on file.

Cover design by Paul Qualcom

Print ISBN: 978-1-5107-4086-0
Ebook ISBN: 978-1-5107-4087-7

Printed in the United States of America.

This book is dedicated to my children, Aron, Benjamin, and Natalie, who are the lights of my life and the inspiration for all I do. To my father, the teacher, who drives my thirst to keep learning and to continue bringing educational opportunities to those in need. I also dedicate this book to my Mum, who gave me a sense of self and a desire to welcome others "into my tent."

CONTENTS

ACKNOWLEDGMENTS

I want to thank so many people who helped me along the way, starting with my brother, Terry, for having absolute faith in my capabilities and confidence. He truly put the wind in my sails. Thank you to my other dear siblings: Sue, David, Ben, Uri, Rebecca, and Sophie and all my incredible, loving nieces and nephews with whom I have lifelong connections. To my father, Aba Nagi, who has been the greatest influence in my life, I thank you for everything. Thank you to my children, Aron, Ben, and Natalie: you inspire me the most, every day.

I also owe so much to Joan Giles, the buyer at Rockmans department stores. She propelled us to stardom. The power of one individual can make all the difference in the world. Thanks to Joan, I learned the importance of having persistence and dreaming big.

My appreciation extends to Barbara Shore, event manager extraordinaire, whom I met at one of her first events at one of my hotels thirty years ago. She encouraged me to write this book and introduced me to bestselling author Mark Bego.

I would like to thank Joy Berry, our COO, who has inspired and supported me to maintain the highest level of excellence in hospitality. Thanks to William Cygnor for navigating the numbers as our CFO,

Kerry Cooper, our Director of Operations, and Bianca Barga, our VP of Membership, Performance and Distribution. To my super sales team that includes Michelle Freedman, VP of Global Sales, Lucy Alvarez, Evan Anderson, Lmi Unson, and Miranda Lee—I appreciate all your efforts and hard work. Thank you to Adrienne Crag-Aziz, Aaron Peaslee, Chef Olivier Rouselle, Judith Feldman, Hudith Castro, Alberto Mendez, Lulu Juarez, and Bobby Kuhns for their dedication to the Luxe Rodeo Drive and Sunset Boulevard hotels. To the Luxe Hotels and Luxe Collection international team members, Melissa Brown in New York, Lisa Iaquez in Florida, Fiona Rose in Australia, Nicoletta Pillardi in London, Gonzalo Ocejo and Patricia Rubiano in Madrid, Adeline Surault in Italy, Sylvia Fletcher in Frankfurt, Mauricio Menendez in South America, and Garrick Yang in Shanghai, you are the incredible colleagues who continue to forge ahead and create a revolution in the hospitality industry. I thank my entire team for their dedication and continued loyalty throughout all these years. I also want to acknowledge all the former employees who, over the years, have added to the layers of our success with their expertise.

Thank you to Joel Fishman, Neil Schwartz, and Shel Brucker, my business mentor and personal friends, respectively. To the late Paul Pollack, who is survived by his daughter, Eileen, and her husband, Charlie Weber, I appreciate their patience and support in numerous Los Angeles City Council hearings. The Pollack home is adjacent to my hotel property in Bel Air, and he and his family gave the term "love thy neighbor" a totally new meaning for me. My gratitude goes out to Dr. Wesley and Pat Moore for their support as our Sunset Hotel next-door neighbors.

I would like to acknowledge my friends and family for their continued love and support: Joanne Novell, John Aguilar, Riny Punderika, Kami Soltani, Angie and Moise Hendeles, Laibl Wolf, Philip Diskin, David and Louise Elias, Moshe Benzaquen, Paul Mir, Kam and Lily

Babaoff, Sheri Rashidi, Fred and Dina Leeds, Vera and Brian Liebenthal, Marty Cooper, David Weiss, Eric Abelev, Jonathan Tessler, Rich Reinis, Rick Richman, Jackie Harell, Vince Calcagno, Tony Gronroos, Agustin Garza, Neel Muller, Karen Fisher, and Jac and Carol Stulberg. I also would like to thank everyone at Harkham-GAON Academy—Dr. Debora Parks, Yosef Miller, and the rest of the dedicated and talented administration shaping the next generations of our leaders.

A special thank you to my very good friend Todd Black, who is blessed with the gift of empathy and really helped me become aware of my context, for which I will always be grateful. Jordana Miller, thank you for your continued friendship and help with this book. I appreciate my nephew, Richie Harkham, for partnering with me at Harkham Wines and the Hark Angel Foundation, where we have built schools in impoverished countries serving over 1,500 children. Thank you to Yigal Kutai for your friendship and wisdom. I am very grateful to Deborah Roberts for her patience, care, and support through this incredible process.

To Mark Bego, who has been on this extraordinary journey with me in helping me put my story together, and David Marken in leading the way to get this book picked up, I thank you for your dedicated efforts and unrelenting guidance. I am forever indebted to Jay Cassell at Skyhorse for believing in the story and encouraging me to shape it. Sarah Clark, thank you so much for all your detailed work on the manuscript and all your assistance in making this book happen. I am proud to say that all of my proceeds from the sale of this book will go to the Hark Angel Foundation.

Preface

MEET EFREM HARKHAM, ROCK STAR HOTELIER

BY MARK BEGO

You are probably wondering why a best-selling rock 'n' roll author such as myself is writing a book about a successful businessman in the hotel world. Well, the answer is quite simply because Efrem Harkham is truly a rock star among international hoteliers!

Although Efrem Harkham's name might not be instantly recognizable to you, he owns Luxe Hotels, a brand consisting of luxurious world class hotels in Los Angeles and beyond. The brand's collection includes the Luxe Sunset Boulevard Hotel in Brentwood, the Luxe Rodeo Drive Hotel in Beverly Hills, the Luxe City Center Hotel in downtown Los Angeles, and the Luxe Rose Garden Hotel in Rome, Italy. He also launched another group of affiliated luxury hotels known as the Luxe Collection—a boutique hotel sales and marketing company representing a collection of over seventy prestigious hotels located around the world.

Efrem began his career in the fashion business in Australia. From there, he almost instantly tapped into his true talent as a marketing master. His first business adventure was a successful run with Sydney-based Lulu Fashions, which—under his co-ownership—became a multi-million-dollar apparel brand. When he moved to Los Angeles in the 1980s, he became the co-owner of Jonathan Martin fashions. In addition, he has been the producer of feature films including *Gorky Park*, and he is a partner in a successful family winery in Hunter Valley, to the north of Sydney, Australia.

But the hospitality industry is where he really shines. It was during his successful run with Jonathan Martin women's clothing line that Harkham first became involved in the hotel business. His initial property, the Luxe Sunset Boulevard Hotel in Bel Air, blossomed into a gem among hotels, becoming Efrem's prototype for his group of hotels that exude comfort, appeal, convenience, and generous hospitality.

Over the years, the Luxe Sunset Boulevard Hotel has become an exclusive destination that even rock stars such as the Rolling Stones liked to stay at because of its privacy, service, and understated luxury. He then branched out with his creation and ownership of the Luxe Rodeo Drive Hotel in Beverly Hills, at a legendary site where the Beatles once stayed and performed. Now that's what I call rock 'n' roll credibility! Today, the Luxe Rodeo Drive Hotel is a sought-after Los Angeles destination for an international clientele who want to stay in the middle of the fashionable Beverly Hills / Rodeo Drive action.

When I first met Efrem in 2014, I was immediately impressed with his sincerity and graciousness. As I listened to him tell his unique story, hearing him modestly discussing his accomplishments, I was greatly intrigued to find out what makes him tick. I was fascinated to hear tales of his drive, his dreams, his family history, and his many accomplishments. While Efrem was still in his twenties and only having recently arrived in the United States, he made his first million dollars and moved to Beverly Hills. Only four years after arriving in the United States, he paid in cash to purchase the car of his dreams: a Corniche Rolls Royce. Now that's what I call a dramatic entry into America. After that came Efrem's initial launch into the hotel business. Listening to him recall his start, I was amazed to hear him tell his inspirational stories to me, and it made me want to be his partner in telling his fascinating story.

Not only is he an instinctive and masterful businessman, but along the way Efrem's spiritual journey became a large reason for the centered natural confidence and enthusiasm that he exudes. He started his life in the Jewish religion, but when he arrived in California he stretched out and embraced Zen Buddhism and yoga. Efrem eventually found that Judaism presented the best spiritual path for him to take, yet he retains the meditative teachings he learned from his Zen guru and he still practices yoga.

Efrem's story has many interesting facets. He has a deep appreciation of art, a gracious desire to make people feel at home, and a passionate love of education. To meet his needs of giving back to the community, he has established schools and educational programs in America, Asia, and Africa. According to him, he learned the concept of hospitality from his mother, and inherited his appreciation for education from his teacher father. As I have gotten to know him, I can honestly say that he exudes the perfect mixture of both passions.

For Efrem, hospitality isn't a job, it's a way of life; it's his calling. When I first went to meet with him at his home to start working on this book, I was delighted to be offered exotic and soothing teas and freshly baked cookies, and inhale the smells of cinnamon, cardamom, and almonds emanating from a welcoming kitchen. It was nothing less than a warm and inviting experience. According to Efrem, that is what walking into his mother's home was like. This is the welcoming kind of hospitality that he strives to replicate in boutique hotels around the world. This kind of "gracious host" nature has become the hallmark of Efrem's Luxe Hotels.

What you will find on these pages is part memoir, part business-oriented book, and part insightful guide to self-help and self-empowerment. Here Efrem shares his favorite inspirations and philosophies for achieving personal success. Efrem's many life lessons underscore the importance of setting and attaining goals, not losing focus, and having unwavering perseverance. These are all concepts that resonated with me, and I am certain you will find them enlightening too.

This book is the tale of someone who comes from modest beginnings, yet was able to come to the United States to create a business world of his own, based on his own sense of incomparable graciousness. As a hotelier, Efrem Harkham has the drive, the passion, and the natural desire to take generous hospitality at his hotels to a new plateau. He is also the epitome of living the American dream and doing things his way. He also takes time to give back through his philanthropic initiatives.

And so, I would like to introduce you to Efrem Harkham—hotel owner, art lover, educator, host, vintner, visionary, and sincere friend. Come along on his journey and look into his world. It is an experience I like to think of as "Living the Luxe Life."

Introduction

SHOWING UP IS EVERYTHING

BY EFREM HARKHAM

I often feel like I'm going through a tunnel, heading for the light. At other times, I am the light and others are following me through the tunnel. Whether it was at school, in my marriage, or as a parent, an employer, or a son, it's dark and sometimes frightening in that tunnel. But getting through it, and emerging into the light, is always the goal. It's about how we come through each tunnel we encounter that counts. Are we kinder, wiser, stronger, empowered, and confident for having made it to the other side? My lifelong quest for success has changed direction dramatically over the years. In this book, I chronicle these successes and challenges I've encountered in the hope of inspiring others to reach for their dreams.

At a young age, I was focused on accomplishing my goals: earning my first million dollars, moving to Los Angeles, and even buying a Rolls Royce. I attained all those goals by age twenty-five, but it left me wondering. Over the years, I learned that these material goals were somewhat satisfying, but not really important in the overall scheme of things.

After moving to Los Angeles, I was going to Mexico to check on our clothing production factory. On my return from Tijuana, I lost control of my car and it went over the center divider and hit another car in a head-on collision. It was a near fatal incident. The steering wheel jammed into me and cut my stomach, causing massive internal bleeding. My stomach surged with blood, my large and small intestines were lacerated, and my spleen had to be removed. The ambulance took me to the Chula Vista Medical Center in San Diego, where my surgeon said that if I had not been attended to within fifteen minutes, I would have bled to death. I know I was very lucky that day and it was a big turning point for me. I realized the value of life, appreciating everything with greater intensity, after this experience. I was feeling my smallness, having felt invincible before. It made me want to become a better person, professionally, personally, and spiritually. So, I set out on a personal development quest.

I moved from Australia to Los Angeles in 1978 to pursue my dreams. My first endeavor in the business world was in the apparel industry. I also invested in real estate, and once that was successful, I sold my interest in the clothing company. It was at that juncture that I got the hospitality bug.

My success in the hotel business was not planned. My parents didn't finance my career because they didn't have the financial capacity to do so. I had to create my own success, and one main reason for doing so was to support my parents. Ultimately, that's what drove me—knowing they needed financial support. I always felt this was my responsibility.

My real estate ventures began with some properties in downtown LA, Beverly Hills, and Brentwood. Subsequently, I purchased the seven-acre Bel Air Sands Hotel on Sunset Boulevard, and I started to provide the "home away from home" experience for my guests. The Luxe Hotels brand has as its purpose the goal of providing a memorable experience, from beginning to end. I fully embraced and embodied the "Luxe" Hotels concept. I love this four-letter word!

What is "The Luxe Life?" Merriam-Webster's dictionary claims the word "luxe" is synonymous with "luxurious." In my definition, the word "luxe" symbolizes all that is positive. To me, the word conjures up the attributes of "light," "hospitality," "kindness," "generosity," "warmth," and "respect." There is nothing more "luxurious" than to be able to treat people in that fashion and to be treated that way in return. Everyone wants to feel pampered and cared about. When kindness is extended unquestioningly, you will find these same caring emotions stirring within you. What is more "luxe" than to feel appreciated? To live an existence where we all appreciate and care about each other, that is what "Living the Luxe Life" is all about.

Before founding Luxe Hotels, my experience with franchises, and being associated with a large hotel chain, was negative. But luckily, I believed there was room for one more player in the hotel world. One that would keep its promises! In this book I highlight the wisdom, philosophies, and great minds of biblical Abraham, the forefather of hospitality, legendary basketball coach John Wooden, the positive psychologist Victor Frankl, author and Yale professor Steve Carter, and Dale Carnegie's Golden Rules of *How to Win Friends and Influence People*.

Everything important that has happened throughout both my childhood and adulthood boils down to "showing up." Even in the business world, every big occurrence amounted to being there and making an effort to "show up." Throughout this book, I intend to demonstrate the importance of "showing up" and making myself available for opportunities that come my way. When I recently spent time with my three kids on Father's Day, they described to me how they are "showing up" in their own lives. I was delighted to hear that some of my lessons are rubbing off on them. My hope is that some of my lessons will rub off on you. Keep in mind: while terrible things may happen in life, getting up every day and "showing up" with the goal of accomplishing something good in the world will help you muddle through until you can once again see the light.

Along the way, there are people we must take care of in life. I had a close friend named Golda. I took care of her until she passed away at age ninety-nine. From the time my son, Aron, was three years old to the time he was eight, I would take him over to Golda's apartment on Ocean Boulevard in Santa Monica. We would drive Golda to do her grocery shopping every Friday morning. Taking care of her was an example of practicing civility and kindness in my own life. While working hard building my business, I also took the time to aid certain individuals like Golda. These acts of kindness ultimately helped me maintain my sanity. It gave my life meaning, and it made it palatable to work hard during the week, knowing I'd soon go and take care of others before the weekend came—the joy of doing good deeds.

Please sit back and join me as I recount my journey from my challenging beginnings in an Israeli refugee camp, to a fulfilling life I worked hard to build in Beverly Hills, California. I continue to grow and learn as I navigate the four key elements—or pillars—of my life: Family, Business, Parenting, and Inspiration. Welcome to my world!

PILLAR ONE
FAMILY

"What you get by achieving your goals is not as important as what you become by achieving your goals."

—Henry David Thoreau

Chapter 1

GENESIS

THE TOMB OF EZRA

My mother's family is from Al-Uzair, a city in Iraq located on the western shore of the Tigris, approximately sixty miles north of Basra. For generations, they were the caretakers of the tomb of the prophet, Ezra (480–440 BCE), who died there after completing the reconstruction of the Second Temple. According to several ancient texts, the prophet Ezra selected 24,000 Jewish men from Iraq, and with the approval of Cyrus, the ruler of the Ottoman Empire, he brought them to rebuild King Solomon's Temple in Jerusalem. Once it was completed, Ezra left his men there to encourage the repopulation of Jerusalem. But Ezra didn't want to die in Israel; he wanted to go back to his roots in Iraq. On his journey, he passed away in Al-Uzair, a site where people continue to make pilgrimage to his tomb for prayer and inspiration. That same Tomb of Ezra is still there to this day. Amazingly, the Iraqi family in whose care my grandfather left his entire enterprise, land, and home are still there to this day, maintaining the property and the tomb.

My mother came from an affluent family. In addition to keeping up the Tomb of Ezra, the family attained their wealth by establishing a factory exporting bricks to Europe. Another source of revenue came from their date tree orchards, which were located on the same property.

My father also came from a wealthy Iraqi family. His father, who was born in Turkey, was a successful and well-respected doctor, who also filled in as the community rabbi. There was a room in his house where he performed medical procedures and surgeries. He would recall how people came through each day for a multitude of medical issues.

On many occasions, my grandfather would not charge patients who were unable to afford his services, an act for which the Muslims in his community honored him. People would bring him food, chickens, or other items to pay him for his services. My dad would often tell me and my siblings how he used to worship his dad, my grandfather, and would strive to emulate him or just get close to him.

My father was educated and was sent to a modern American school in Lebanon. My father married my mom at the age of twenty-one and went to live with her family. He basically "changed tents," and moved in with his new wife and her parents.

FROM RICHES TO REFUGEE CAMP

After all these years, I have finally distilled the story my family has told me of that time and place in Iraq over the years. I've also confirmed their stories by my own research of Iraq between 1930 and 1950, as well as my knowledge of the 1948 founding of Israel. My parents and grandparents made it our generation's duty to tell their intricate and deep-rooted story.

What follows is a condensed sequence of events pertaining to why Iraq has been embattled for thousands of years. Historically, the area was called Babylonia, or Mesopotamia. This is the birthplace of Abraham, who began a movement of deep religious faith and kindness toward others' welfare. He was recognized and revered by the Judaic, Christian, and Muslim faiths. He taught that serving God and offering hospitality to others were not two separate things, but one. Prior to Abraham's revelation of monotheism, people used to sacrifice children and worship forces of nature, like the stars and the sun, as gods. God was beyond nature. Abraham is one of my favorite characters in the Bible. His teachings about seeing a trace of God in the face of a stranger had a major impact on me. This learning has perfected my capacity to respect and appreciate the beauty and uniqueness of the thousands of people my hospitality team and I host every day in our groups of hotels.

Abraham received a divine calling to uproot himself and his wife Sarah from his birthplace in Mesopotamia. He blindly accepted the divine power's instruction to go to the Promised Land—Canaan, which was later to be called Israel.

Approximately 1,500 years later, Abraham's descendent, King Solomon, built a majestic first temple to house God's *shekinah* (divine presence) in Jerusalem. In 750 BCE, the Assyrians destroyed this temple. All Jews who inhabited Canaan were driven out. Many sojourned to neighboring Babylon, which became the center for Judaic wisdom and learning.

King Cyrus of the Ottoman Empire acquiesced to the request of the prophet Ezra, who was living in Iraq, to rebuild the holy temple in Jerusalem. Ezra selected 24,000 men to trek back to accomplish this task. The mission was accomplished, and the governor appointed by Rome's Caesar, King Herod, made the finishing touches.

In 70 CE the temple was burned and destroyed by the Romans. Again, all those Jews living in the area, now renamed by the Romans as Palaestina, were exiled once more to many surrounding countries. My ancestors resettled in the ancient city of Basra in Babylon, with a population of approximately 200,000 Jews.

Fast-forward to modern-day Iraq. Iraq was established after WWI in 1919 by the League of Nations when the Ottoman Empire fell on the losing side of the war. Turkish Iraq was then placed under the authority of the British, with a monarchy established in 1921. Faisal I, who fought alongside the famed Lawrence of Arabia, was designated king of Iraq. Under Faisal's rule, the Jewish population was given full rights as Iraqi citizens. This social status of the Jews continued even after Iraq gained independence from the British in 1932.

When Nazi propaganda reached Iraq, Hitler's *Mein Kampf* was translated into Arabic. Pro-Nazi youth movements soon became more visible in public places, gaining traction and gradually influencing the political climate in Iraq.

A pro-Nazi cleric, Haj Muhammad Amin Al-Hussein, came to Iraq in 1936 from Palestine to collaborate with Nazi Germany on a plot to overthrow the Iraqi king. This cleric promised Hitler oil in exchange for the destruction of all the Jews in Iraq, first, and eventually in the entire region of the Middle East. Despite the warning signs, my parents, like a large portion of the Jewish community in Iraq, did not believe that Hitler's Nazi regime would have the capability of uprooting them after living there for over two thousand years.

In April 1941, a nationwide anti-British coup took place. It was short-lived, however, since within one month, the British Army was able to restore order and put down the takeover and reinstate the British-backed king.

Frustrated by the failure of the coup, nationalist Iraqi soldiers and civilians were soon exposed to a barrage of anti-Israel and anti-Jewish propaganda on the streets, on the radio, and in the mosques. Mufti Haj Amin al-Husseini accused the entire Jewish community in Iraq of being spies. Suddenly, a bloody uprising erupted against a delegation of Jewish dignitaries, who were en route to greet the homecoming king. This unleashed thirty hours of constant barrage against the Jews of Iraq, an attack which was eventually called Farhoud.

The pogrom took place on a Jewish holiday called Shavuot and lasted two days. Hundreds of Jewish homes, businesses, and synagogues were broken into and looted. Before it was over, 180 Jews were murdered and over 200 were maimed or wounded. My father and his family members locked themselves in one of their houses, where they witnessed the horrible atrocities. Luckily my entire family and their holdings were unharmed.

The community continued with their lives after this episode, hoping that things would return to normal. Neighbors assisted their fellow Jews who were impacted by the riots and helped to rebuild Jewish schools and synagogues.

The community breathed a collective sigh of relief in early September 1945 when the war came to an end. It began to feel like the community could once again co-exist.

On November 29, 1947, a resolution was miraculously passed by a majority at the UN to terminate the British mandate and allow for an independent Jewish and Arab state to be recognized. After 2,000 years of Jews being forcibly exiled from their beloved land and disbursed to the four corners of the globe, they were going to have a land to call their own. People kept the faith throughout the dispersion and never stopped praying and hoping for their return. In implementing the 1947 UN resolution, a secret invitation was sent to 200 guests to attend a ceremony at 4:00 p.m. on Friday, May 14, 1948 announcing the declaration of Israel's independence. This was done in secret because they feared that the British or the Arabs might thwart the occasion. On the same day, my mom gave birth to her fourth child, my brother Uri. The joy over the simultaneous birth of the state and a baby boy was overshadowed the next day, on May 15, by a joint declaration of war against Israel by Iraq, Egypt, Jordan, Saudi Arabia, and Syria.

Miraculously, Israel succeeded in pushing back the Iraqi and other forces, despite its meager military arsenal and limited infantry. This defeat was a major embarrassment to the Iraqi royal family and the leaders of Egypt, Jordan, Saudi Arabia, and Syria.

The Iraqi government took measures to take away some of the privileges previously given to the Jewish population in Iraq. An incident took place at this time that shocked the Jewish population; it is a story my dad has repeated to me on numerous occasions.

Shafiq Ades, an Iraqi Jewish businessman who imported Ford cars to Iraq, was a very close friend of the king and other influential politicians. Thus, Ades was chosen as a convenient target for the Iraqis who were venting feelings of revenge toward Israel and the Jewish population. Local newspapers, which were supported by the people, began a horrific smear campaign against Ades. He was arrested on false charges of shipping arms to Israel. At his trial, he was found guilty of treason. All his assets were confiscated by the government and he was be sentenced to death.

King Faisal signed the court ruling after three days of uncertainty and painful deliberations. (After all, Shafiq was a supporter, confidante, and a personal friend to the king.) My dad recounts the exact wording of what Prime Minister Sayid Mohamed told the king: "Either you hang this Jew and save your chair, or you lose your chair for the Jew's sake." On hearing these words, King Faisal signed the document, approving the death sentence.

The trial and hanging of Shafiq Ades was a major blow to my father and the Jewish community as a whole. My dad recalls that the hanging was turned into a spectacle in the city square. The crowd was so large that the executors had to hang Shafiq twice on the same day, first at 8:00 a.m. and then again at 10:00 a.m.

This was to be a major signal to the Jews that they were no longer welcome. There were massive layoffs of Jewish government employees. Rather than undergo the trauma ahead, many preemptively decided to convert to Islam. Others changed their names slightly to sound more Arabic. Dad proudly says that it never crossed his mind to just assimilate.

The environment for the Jewish community in Iraq in 1950 and 1951 was a state of mayhem. They were scrambling to make sense of the situation. The government began to nationalize businesses owned by Jews that were registered to emigrate from Iraq. Approximately ten thousand Jews per month were leaving the country—many by trains and buses via Iran. The Mossad, Israel's national intelligence agency, struck a deal with the Iraqi prime minister to land its planes in the Basra airfields and bring its new citizens to safety, at a price of fifty pounds sterling per Jew. The community began to crumble around them. Their hope that everything would eventually change and go back to the way things used to be was no longer a reality.

My parents were among the last groups of Jews to leave Iraq in April 1951. The departure experience left emotional scars for many. At the airport, every individual, adults and children, were body searched to ensure they were not smuggling cash or jewelry out of the country. My older sister Sue, approximately six years old at the time, recalls arguing with an Iraqi airport official who noticed a gold ring on her finger. She had no choice but to hand it to the guard.

Departure rules were extremely strict. Every passenger was allowed to bring on board only five pounds in weight, which was to include only personal effects, such as clothes and photographs; there were no exceptions to this law. My parents, Sue, brothers David, Ben, Uri, and Terry, both grandmothers, and my grandfather boarded the plane. They then watched as the plane took off, realizing that their lives would never be the same again. The land that had been their home their entire lives, the place that they loved so much, had turned into a chaotic environment from which they had to flee. It was a devastating and shocking event for all to endure.

The Promised Land of Israel, despite the longing to be back to the land from which our ancestors were expelled by the Romans over two thousand years prior, was unattractive to my parents and they were even uncertain whether Israel could survive this huge migration of people. Being forced to give up their history, belongings, professions, and the life they loved created an overwhelming sense of frustration and anger in my parents and their community.

As they approached Israel, my parents did not anticipate the mayhem they encountered upon landing. The first order of business was to spray all new arrivals with DDT, a commonly used pesticide for insect control. Then nurses began a lice check. This airport experience threw my mother into a state of silence—she became depressed and lost her desire to talk with anyone. Israel had become increasingly crowded.

In the five years prior to my family's arrival in 1951, Israel had already absorbed over 700,000 Jewish refugees. Israel's population prior to this influx was approximately 600,000 people. This was a huge undertaking for a newly created nation. Insufficient housing and food shortages were major problems, and the Iraqi authorities had hoped Israel would simply collapse under this pressure.

After my dad completed all the bureaucratic details at the airport on behalf of the entire family, they were directed toward rows of trucks awaiting their arrival in the middle of the night. The young and the old grandmothers clambered onto the uncovered trucks for a two-hour journey, all the while not knowing where their destination would be. They finally arrived at Binyamina, where I was born. It is located out in the hinterlands of Israel, in a mountainous area, just south of Haifa and north of Tel Aviv. Nowadays, it is regarded as a lush and desirable area, but back then it was essentially in the middle of nowhere.

My family and over 100,000 other refugees were placed in old British military camps. Here, they erected tents and ramshackle corrugated, sheet-metal huts. In the years after, my mom would often speak of the muddy conditions, the chaotic environment, the unseemly outdoor communal toilets and showers. My mom, who loved to cook exotic and complicated dishes, found herself dealing with ration coupons for eggs, milk, and bread.

Israel, during this time, was in a deep economic crisis. The harsh rationing implemented by the government in 1949 did not help the situation. The government could not repay its debt. Inflation was over 30 percent, the economy was close to collapsing, and there was a severe food shortage due to the huge population influx into the newly formed country.

There was no other solution but to persevere. My father had to do all that he could to ensure the family survived living in this refugee camp for the next four years. Many families were not as fortunate as we were. The camps were prone to diseases. Many infant children, taken from the parents to be treated in the makeshift infirmary, were permanently separated from their families and adopted out to grow up in cleaner and more established communities. My mom, aware that this was a possibility, made sure she never took her eyes off her children, especially when they were ill.

My parents survived this ordeal, I believe, primarily due to their deep-rooted faith. They were pragmatic and saw their surroundings exactly as they were and not how they would like them to be. They never gave up hope that they could and would make it better, one step at a time. My parents believed that we are on earth for a reason, and that in our journey through life, God is always with us. Mom's mantra to me and my siblings in Arabic was *Allah Wiyakim*, meaning God is always with you, helping us rise when we fall, and that God believes in us more than we believe in ourselves.

It is this faith that allowed my parents and grandparents to live in such perpetual uncertainty. It is also this *Emunah*, this faith, which made them certain they would overcome the loss of everything that they left behind in Baghdad. It made them hopeful that they would make it all over again.

I learned from my parents' hardships in those early years that we have the ability to create the atmosphere that surrounds us; that whatever the circumstance, how the world treats us reflects how we behave in the world.

Despite my parents' dire circumstances, they did not become downhearted. They did not give up and just accept the squalor and mess. Through the entire ordeal, my mother continued to ensure her family had food despite the rations. Soon after arriving in Israel, she went to the local market, and with the little money that she had, bought two chickens. The family no longer depended on the egg coupons, and focused on the meat and chicken coupons, which were harder to get. According to my older sister Sue, who was six at the time, Mom would use the chicken or meat from the coupons in various dishes to maximize its use and prolong the family's meat intake. Within a few months, Mom got a goat. Not only was my family enjoying the fresh goat milk, my mom would make Sue and David deliver bottles of goat milk to family and friends living near us. This way, they made the most out of the little they were given.

Due to my parents' examples during these years, I learned that when things are at their worst, you should try to make things better around you. That's still how I handle adversity in my life. As Jews, we are constantly taught the reason God tests us with adversity is because God wants us to develop to our fullest potential. When we undergo the "test," we are certain that we have the ability to handle it and to pass it with flying colors. We must remember that our abilities are greater than we can imagine. As Mahatma Gandhi reminds us, "Strength does not come from winning. Your struggles develop your strengths. When you go through hardships and decide not to surrender, that is strength."

In those difficult years when my parents were in the impoverished camps, they brooded over their misery for a bit, but then took full responsibility for their situation and began to pull themselves together.

They both set clear, defined, concrete, and tangible goals. Mom was entirely focused on ensuring the children had sufficient food and warm and clean clothes. Her eyes were set on moving out of the squalor.

My dad fixated on something larger scale, namely the inadequate education program being offered to the children in grades one through twelve. He saw the unfortunate circumstances surrounding the inadequate and lacking schooling system. He ultimately succeeded in creating the educational model he wanted. He was able to move past his circumstances and work toward making the world around him better.

His favorite memory was the joy on the school children's faces when he arranged to distribute a daily small lunch package that included a small bottle of milk and a fresh bread roll. Even though 90 percent of the people could not pay for this, he managed to sustain this lunch program the entire time he was associated with the school. The kids, including me, were so grateful for this treat because for some of us it meant that we were not overwhelmed with hunger during the school day.

It's easy to get discouraged when things are going bad. We should not lose heart. As shown in the movie *Cast Away* with Tom Hanks, remember that the next time your little hut seems to be burning to the ground, it may just be a smoke signal, in fact. It may just be the best thing that has happened!

Remember that if you plant poison, you get poison. If you plant great stuff, innovative thoughts, and positive ideas, it grows as such. Our minds are fertile ground, and so whatever you put in is what you get out. The lentil will come back to you tenfold. That is a very basic thought, yet such a powerful insight. My parents constantly told us that things would get better, and we believed them. Today my family's legacy of success and bringing kindness into the world lives on.

A PURIM TO REMEMBER

One of the most important lessons from my parents' experience is that despite all the hardships, it is possible to live differently from the way we have been living in the past. It's obviously possible to start over again. It's never too late to be able to undergo change. It's what we evolve into every time change happens that matters. Adults have the duty to do the right thing, even if it's against logic. Whatever the situation, it is our duty to make responsible life decisions—not doing a half-hearted job or leaving loose ends that come back to haunt us and which cause untold damage both financially and emotionally.

As my father vividly illustrates, he and his family did their best to always find reasons to be happy. My father and mother certainly did not have an easy life. He wrote about the early days in Israel in his 2011 book *Beginning in Babylon*.

It is the beginning of spring. There is a cool breeze about, and the air is fragrant. It was the spring, with its feeling of renewal, which took me back to another birth, a long time ago. Your birth, my dear son, took place on the festival of Purim, so many years ago, but I still remember it is as though it were yesterday.

I remember the moment that the messenger came to the synagogue, to inform me that your mother had gone into labor. It was just as we had finished reading the *Megillat Esther (The Book of Esther)*. I left the synagogue anxiously. Within a few minutes your mother and I were on our way in the ambulance to the maternity hospital in Hadera. It was only a short time after we got there that the midwife came out with a smile on her face, to congratulate me on your birth.

Purim is usually a joyful time in our family, as it is for all Jews, but that day the joy was many times greater. Your brothers and sisters put on the colorful costumes, that your mother had prepared before she gave birth, and so Queen Esther, King Ahashverosh, a clown, a magician and a dancer all sang and celebrated the arrival of their newest brother into the world . . . The children were thrilled to be joined by their new brother. The older children begged us to name him Ephraim, excited to complete the biblical pair that were blessed in the Torah, "Menashe and Ephraim."

In spite of our excitement, we did not forget the more serious obligations of the day, to send gifts of food to our friends. After, the first outburst of happiness, the children set out, each one carrying a plate loaded with sweets and fruit, to wish our friends a happy day and to inform them of the new baby who had joined our family . . .

My father went on to write this about me in his book:

Today I am talking to you man-to-man, but my memory goes back to when you were but a child, when we would go for walks to the Carmel hills, and I would carry you on my shoulders (as I did all of your brothers and sisters). We used to sing together then and although we weren't rich, we were certainly happy and united. I may not have showered you with kisses when you were children, because I thought that spoiled children didn't learn to cope with the challenges that life throws at them, but I loved you very much. I still do.

Efrem, we appreciate you, you are our dear son, a goodhearted lad, may you grow and continue to lead with your loving nature, and may God give you everything you want.

MY SIBLINGS

My siblings have been an integral part of my life, and so deserve their own introduction. First comes my eldest sister, Sue. She married her husband, David, whom she met in Israel. He is a quiet man, but he is a great builder and has a million stories about his experiences of escaping

Iraq by train and on foot when he was only thirteen years old. Sue and David live in Los Angeles and have four children. Sue is a successful fashion designer for her company called Siena Rose.

Then there is my brother Mordechai, named after our grandfather. Upon arriving in Australia, he anglicized his name to David. He is the second child and was the first one to move from Israel to Australia.

When he was seventeen, my dad arranged for David to immigrate to Australia so he would not have to serve as a soldier in the Israeli Defense Force. David started us out in the fashion business when he opened the family's first fashion shop in Sydney. He and his wife, Israela, live in Los Angeles and have four children.

Next is Ben, who is a lawyer and a successful real estate developer. He is my only sibling to have served in the Israeli Defense Forces. Ben and his wife, Sharon, live in Australia. They have six children.

Since my brother Uri was born next, on Israel's Independence Day, May 14, 1948, he is very connected to Israel and its leaders. Uri has a very powerful personality and is the center of attention at every gathering. He has six children and lives in Beverly Hills.

Menashe, who later anglicized his name to Terry, is involved in real estate. We worked together in the garment industry and I learned a lot from him. Terry and his wife, Geraldine, have nine children and live in Australia. Terry's son, Richie, runs Harkham Wines in the Hunter Valley of Australia, which will be discussed later in the book. I am very close to all my siblings' children and grandchildren, even though we live so far away from each other.

All of my siblings just mentioned were born in Iraq. Rebecca, my second oldest sister, was the first sibling to be born in Israel. She moved to Los Angeles about ten years ago. Rebecca met her husband Anthony, whose family were regular guests at our home in Sydney for festive Jewish holidays and numerous Shabbat dinners. Anthony's dad was a successful manufacturer who supplied David's stores with casual dresses. They are blissfully married for over forty years and have three children. Their calling in Australia and in the US is to provide quality sober living accommodations for people overcoming drug and alcohol addictions and who are not ready to return to their life at home after drug rehab treatment programs. They live in Los Angeles.

I come next in line.

Finally, there is Sophie, my younger sister, who also lives in Los Angeles. She is on a mission to become a yoga and mindfulness instructor. She has two children.

We are a very close family and attend all of our family celebrations together. We will be celebrating my father's 105th birthday together this year. When people ask my dad what he attributes his longevity to, he always repeats, "When you throw a lentil in the water, it will come back to you at some point in your life."

THEY TOLD US WE CAME FROM ROYALTY

My father and mother always told my siblings and me that, in spite of the tough living situation that we found ourselves in, wherever we lived, we were royalty. I grew up believing that.

I think my parents truly believed that we were part of the royal line, but I also think they were giving us hope. They told us lots of stories and gave everything a positive spin. They told us God has a plan, so we should have faith and things would eventually get better. We all believed it. I was told biblical stories, as if I were part of them, and my siblings and I believed them. We believed we were a very integral part of a grand story. Otherwise our lives would not have had meaning.

Throughout my impoverished childhood, I kept telling myself that I would somehow rise above all of this. I had no idea if someone was going to miraculously come save us. I was so confused as to exactly what was going to happen. But I knew that I was from good stock, and that something better was coming.

This stagnation pervaded most areas of my life. In school I found that I was unable to learn. My mind was always elsewhere. I deeply felt my parents' pain. These were tough days they went through, and I was aware of it.

There was one day of the week that I longed for and it made life worthwhile: Shabbat, Friday night and the entire day Saturday. Shabbat continues to be the time I most remember from my youth. The aroma of all the delicious food my mom would prepare for hours—it was an event, a real banquet, always complete with delicious challah bread, grape wine, and the beautiful smell and taste of the juice.

Wherever we lived, we always celebrated all the Jewish holidays, including Passover, Purim, Shavuot, Rosh Hashanah, Sukkot, and Hanukkah, Friday night and Shabbat day. It was always so powerful to have eight kids around the table, along with our parents and grand-mother. My favorite was the singing part of the meal. I was always amazed at how my older brothers and sisters knew the words to so many Hebrew folk songs. At those dinners, everyone always looked so clean and wore their finest clothing to experience "Oneg Shabbat"—Ultimate Joy of Shabbat. I thank God for giving me Sabbath on all those years past.

MOTIVATED BY POVERTY

When my parents moved out of the refugee camp Maabara in Binyamina in 1956, they moved into a newly built housing project provided by the government in a neighboring city called Zikhron Ya'akov. The community had a secular public school, but there was no religious school for the primarily Sephardic Jews from Morocco and Turkey to attend. My father was concerned that the secular public school did not teach traditional Jewish values. As a result, he successfully fought to build a religious school which my siblings and I, along with 400 other students, attended.

My mother wanted to buy a house. She convinced my dad to move closer to the city center, insisting that we needed to purchase a home. In addition to the small housing project in Zikhron Ya'akov, my parents bought a small home in Petah Tikva. My mother moved into that house with my grandparents and older siblings. My mother had been displaced from her life of luxury in Iraq, and she was determined to rebuild the life that was once hers. While the rest of the family members lived in apartments, we were one of the rare few to own a house, which was twenty minutes from Tel Aviv. As the home grew in value, my dad was always thankful for that successful investment.

The house was located at the end of a cul-de-sac with a modest backyard, and it backed up to a perfectly lined lush orange orchard. The fragrant blossoms smelled like heaven and nothing tasted sweeter or fresher than fresh oranges. Terry, at thirteen years old, negotiated with Chananya, the owner and farmer of the grove, that during our school vacations, we would pick the crop at harvest time for a couple of shekels per box of oranges. I was nine years old and was Terry's most dedicated picker. I fearlessly climbed tall ladders, equipped with special clippers. Each orange had to be carefully snipped, cutting the stem as short as possible so that it would not damage the other oranges during packing. I recall Terry calling out, "Treat each orange individually and carefully place them in the box. No shortcuts—one orange at a time." I remember how each orange that I picked was different from the others. When they were ripe, they were healthy and thick skinned, feeling heavy in my hand. Those that were lighter, we were instructed to leave on the trees. We created an industry in the backyard that involved my grandmothers, Rebecca, and whoever else that had time to spare. Chananya would count the number of boxes being loaded onto trucks and pay Terry for the cash earned per box, which he happily handed over to my parents.

My older siblings, Sue, David, Ben, and Uri, used the Petah Tikva house. They also went to religious boarding schools and would regularly drop by the centrally located house. My parents decided that my father and the youngest children—myself, Terry, Rebecca, and Sophie—would stay with him in Zikhron Ya'akov to attend his newly built school. What Mom did complain about was that she needed more money. People like her who once had money, and then have had it taken away, always live in fear of not having enough money for the basics—primarily food and meat, which was expensive, and clean clothes for herself and her children.

My father had a different focus. His motivation was to attain more degrees and to engage in higher learning. He knew that the more highly educated he was, the more money he could earn. Plus, he needed more income to support us all.

During the six days of the week that Terry, Rebecca, Sophie, and I spent in Zikhron, we were responsible for ourselves, without adult supervision—miles away from where Mom was living (Petah Tikva). Our neighbors were always generous to invite us and welcome us to eat with their families. Especially so were our dear Moroccan neighbors, Esther and her family. Their food was always absolutely delicious, made and shared with so much love. I recall the fish cooked with lots of tomato juice and onions. The Moroccan people are so warm and hospitable, and I try to emulate their hospitality to my neighbors in my life today.

It truly is a miracle that we made it through this difficult period physically unharmed and all unscathed. I remember several very cold winters in Zikhron Ya'akov. My brother Terry had the idea of burning wood in our little room. Rebecca and I were thankful for the warmth, until the headaches we felt the next morning, because of all the smoke we breathed in the room.

These experiences showed me that my life is about constantly climbing and fighting to get anywhere. I suppose it is where I learned to persevere and to keep pushing ahead, no matter the circumstances. Like Sisyphus, always pushing that proverbial rock up the mountain, I want my children to have that same drive: to be brave, take risks, and to try the bold and daring. I know they will be so thankful that I made them work.

MEMORIES OF MY MOTHER

My mother's welcoming nature stemmed from her family's history of caring for Ezra's Tomb, a site which was entirely open to the public. There was no formal registration or authorization needed to visit the tomb to worship there, so anyone who wanted to be close to the prophet Ezra was welcome. Now that is true hospitality!

I must give my mother all of the credit for teaching me what warmth and gracious hospitality are all about. My mother was the expert. My friends, who actually had the opportunity to experience that warmth, would talk about it. Within seconds of sitting down with my mother, one would be served freshly baked date cookies and fresh tea with mint and cardamom. She was always very warm and welcoming.

To this day I emulate my mom's hospitality with my team at my hotels. I have a strong desire to ensure that people have a positive experience whether they are visiting me in my home in LA, Jerusalem, or coming to stay at one of my hotels, or experiencing a wine tasting experience in the Hunter Valley of Australia. Delighting our guests in the physical environment we create for them, and offering a welcoming, genuine experience from their arrival and throughout their entire time with us, is our goal. Hospitality is ingrained in me.

My parents lived in separate homes in separate cities until the Sabbath every week. We would always get together for the Sabbath on Friday nights in Petah Tikva. Then, we would go back to our one-room home with my father in Zikhron Ya'akov on Sunday morning. We would leave at the crack of dawn because the school week began at 8:00 a.m. on Sunday mornings.

The next big shift was when my mom and dad moved us to Sydney, Australia. My parents, Rebecca, Terry, Sophie, and I left for Australia in 1967, three months prior to the Six-Day War in Israel.

At the time, Australians were extremely tough on foreigners, as they were very much into their own culture. In Australia, Mom was a real foreigner, but she would charm all her Aussie neighbors and they would do favors for her. If we were out of the house and it started raining, the neighbors would go to the backyard, gather up all the laundry that was hanging on the line, fold it up, and leave it in a dry place for her. They absolutely loved her.

I think that Mom was able to charm them because she was authentic. She always gave people the benefit of the doubt—whoever they were. She saw the beauty in others, even if she didn't understand much of what they said. She opened her heart and genuinely welcomed them and showed them her generosity. She valued making people feel special and appreciated.

At the age of thirteen, I took on the task of caring for my mother in Sydney, as her health had begun to take a turn for the worse. My mom couldn't read English. She had only one eye, the result of trachoma, which occurred after she was stuck in a violent wind storm that occurs often in the desert. Untreated as a child, it caused her to lose her sight in that eye. The eye had to be removed, and she had a glass eye for that socket. However, she could not see well from her one remaining eye alone, hence she struggled to read.

I brought my mom by public transportation to the optometrist to fit her with reading glasses, hoping I could teach her the English alphabet. I felt that she deserved to have a good life. I routinely took her to various doctors to alleviate her pain from arthritis and to deal with herniated discs in her back. There was a lot of pain in her back due to calcium deposits. Simply, she had been the washing machine, dishwasher, cook, housecleaner, and everything else for so many people that it eventually took a toll on her health. It seemed like everyone else in the family was very busy with various things to help along, so I jumped in to help my mom.

When I eventually left to move to America, there was no one else to take care of her. She missed her boys when we moved to America, but especially me, because I helped her with all her health issues. Eventually, she and my father made the decision to move to Los Angeles as well. She knew that was going to be good for her.

When she got to the US, I resumed my role of taking care of her. My parents lived in the Luxe Sunset Boulevard Hotel and took up residence there. I arranged to prepare for them two rooms with a kitchen because my mother loved to cook. The hotel smelled delicious! She would always be baking or cooking exotic Iraqi recipes. When I was growing up, there was a certain magic when I would walk into our home, with all the sights, sounds, and smells to grasp. I remember the fragrance of onions and garlic sizzling, and the air filled with the captivating aromas of mint, cinnamon, cardamom, coriander, and fenugreek. I can still remember the lingering sweetness outside of date molasses, freshly ground spices, and Kafi straight from the oven. I cherish my everlasting memories of home with these recipes that date back for centuries, which are delicacies made for our holidays. These were the simple pleasures of life. What beautiful memories come back to me at my own hotel on Sunset Boulevard.

Barbara Shore, a longtime friend, has fond memories of my mom: "Your mother was a wonderful, welcoming woman who was very inspirational. When I would walk into her apartment at the hotel, it was always the best thing that happened all day. She made everyone feel truly special and you couldn't help but love her. She was the kind of person you just wanted to be around. I think that she did a lot to keep everyone together."

Indeed, she did. She was the uniting force in the family for her entire life. She treated every person as a world. She knew their strengths and weaknesses, and she was able to cater to them. My mother was filled with love and lived by the credo: "Love conquers all." In Arabic it is called *mehiba*, an all-encompassing love.

She often had to remind us who we were. I remember one day I was fighting with my brother, and I wanted to kill him. She said, "Come on! Where is the love? Where is the love? Where is the *mehiba*? You are a family. You are princes. You are royalty! How dare you?" And with that, she forced our togetherness. My mother was absolutely brilliant, and she had such a good heart.

I developed my passion for hospitality because of my mom. She didn't speak English well; it was pidgin English at best, but her smile overcame that. In fact, I always tell my hotel employees, "When you see a guest, just smile, and look welcoming! Welcome people with your eyes and warmth. It doesn't matter how poor your English is or if you don't know what a guest is saying in French, just show that you genuinely care with your eyes and expressions because they will speak louder than words."

In an interview with famed painter Marc Chagall, the interviewer said to him, "What drove you to create so much art from such a young age?"

His response: "I wanted to please my mom. I wanted to show her that her vision for me was correct."

A lot of men give all of the credit for their successes to their mom. Moms are powerful, and very often they are the driving forces in their sons' lives. My mother was certainly that to me.

★★★

After a year and a half, my parents were feeling a bit constricted living full-time at the hotel. In 1997, my siblings and I moved them out of the hotel and bought them a house in Beverly Hills on Canon Drive, south of Wilshire Boulevard. My dad lives there to this day. Mom passed away in January 2009. She was eighty-six years old. She was in a lot of pain, but she managed to smile right until the end. As a way to commemorate my mother, I wrote this story about my mother in my dad's book, *Beginning in Babylon* (2011). It read:

> We were all so fortunate to have been placed in this woman's life. She was beautiful and gentle, and yet strong. She was always focused on her family and close friends. She would take care of us children, her mother, and her mother-in-law. Even in Israel when our living space was very restricted and times were tense, she carried us through with firmness and love. She loved her three daughters Sue, Rebecca, and Sophie—and her five sons—David, Ben, Uri, Terry, and me, Efrem.
>
> At all stages of our growing up, she regularly reminded us that we were no ordinary children, and that we were all connected to a very special family that went back to the time of the Prophet Ezra HaSofer.
>
> One of her favorite expressions, when she was talking to a son, was "tihyeh gever," or "be a man." When she was talking to a daughter, she said "tihyie hazaka," or "be strong". She wanted us to be strong and deal with our issues and to have faith that we'll get through a problem. There is no need to get hysterical—that her children and family should not unleash their anger on others but deal with their issues. She had faith that we will have a solution to the issue that is troubling us. At the same time, she taught us to have the utmost compassion for the needy and the old."

I remember that as soon as I started to drive, she put me to good use by having me distribute her delicious smelling food to several elderly people who would always be thrilled to receive Aziza's care packages.

I was always amazed at her ability to cook. She had so many dishes in her repertoire, and into each one she poured her love and care. She loved to have guests over—especially her children and our families, as we got older—sharing, speaking, discussing *Torah*, and singing. Singing always made her happy—especially the old tunes from her childhood, like "Yom ha-Shabbat En Kamohu," and "Dror Yikra." On Shabbats throughout her life, these songs gave her immense peace and inner joy. Towards the last few weeks of her life, she wanted to hear us singing some of the old tunes and she also wanted to hear Tehillim (Psalms) day and night. I was always amazed how she would care about her grandchildren. With my own children she always referred to Natalie as "hasida", meaning wise person. "This is a special girl," she would say, "You should spend more time with Benjamin, he has the best heart and needs to spend quality time with you because he is very sensitive, and Aron, he is just like you—God has enlightened him."

She had a unique way of communicating her love to everyone with whom she came into contact. She is our mentor and we are her legacy.

My mother's giving nature is what all who knew her well remember the most about her. My father, throughout his life, always loved having his family and guests at our homes. Miraculously, no matter the budget he gave my mom for an event, she always made the gathering warm and memorable, as my dad recalls in his memoir *After Babylon*:

Our life settled into a comfortable routine. Every Friday night, our family and various in-laws and friends would gather around our long dining room table for the sumptuous meal. We had fine wine and a repertoire of harmonious traditional Shabbat songs (many of them in the same tunes that were sung in Babylon for many generations).

Aziza would make dish after dish of delectable food: roast chicken, potatoes, pumpkin, kibbeh (ground beef, fried onions and parsley in a semolina shell) in a sweet and sour stew with okra, butternut squash kibbeh in a beetroot stew, potato kibbeh, and rice kibbeh, all fried to a crispy golden perfection. She also made Plau Bjij, rice cooked with chicken and tomato paste, topped with sautéed onion, plump raisins and slivered almonds and Mhasha, a variety of grape leaves, cabbage, onions, and assorted vegetables stuffed with rice and meat.

Aziza prepared all of these ancient delicacies with a light hand and a generous heart. Her table sparkled with fine china and crystal. She was always thrilled to watch her friends and family enjoy the masterpieces she created in the kitchen.

The atmosphere in our home was happy and joyous. There was always the sound of laughter. It was wonderful to watch our children go out into the world and succeed at work and life, and then to always come back to our table.

FATHER'S HIGH EXPECTATIONS

My father always had high expectations of my siblings and me, primarily in academics. He had no time or patience for anything less than perfection in education. His attitude was if he didn't ride his children and push them hard, they would not get results, and so they would fail.

He wanted to know that we were not playing too much, and that we were studying. Whenever he questioned me about my studies, particularly math, my mind would freeze. I would become anxious and scared that he'd be disappointed in me. Unfortunately, over the years, this has been a difficult imprint to shake. I am proud to say I have finally been able to separate my true self from this incorrect perception of myself.

Now that I have experienced being a parent, I see the value of setting expectations for children. Those expectations should force kids to go into high gear in their thinking and perform. With hindsight, I felt I failed my father's expectations of me. He did not provide the tools I required to achieve his goals for me. I needed the basics—warm clothing, a comfortable living environment. I was in a kind of foggy existence during my childhood. I felt sorry for my dad's tough life, so I kept my needs to myself.

My dad worked endlessly while his younger kids lived with him in Zikhron. He completed the school building project, and then pursued his education in the evenings in order to climb the uphill ladder in the Israeli education system. There was no public transportation within Zikhron, so he walked, sometimes biked, everywhere. He would regularly come to our trailer very late, exhausted and often frustrated. We were in bed, keeping quiet, as he prepared to go to bed. We would wake up and he'd already be gone in the morning.

He was driven to earn enough of an income every year and save as much as possible in order to get his immediate family out of Israel. It seems like he was always saving pennies and cutting corners. For example, instead of toilet paper, we used old newspapers.

THE BEDOUIN KIDS

We always had interesting neighbors in Israel. When I was a child growing up there, I sometimes felt that I was living in a jungle. In the early 1960s, when we lived in Zikhron Ya'akov, it was a mountainous,

agricultural area. Bedouins, nomadic Arab people who have historically inhabited the desert regions, lived in the mountains just behind
our community. As kids, my siblings and I became friendly with them,
since my dad often worked as a translator for them. We became friends,
and we would go to their corrugated makeshift tents all the time.

One of the craziest memories about this era of my childhood was the
after-school activities with my brother, Terry, and some Bedouin teenage boys. As mischievous boys, we raced donkeys and cut red hot pep-
pers in half and stuffed them up the behinds of the donkeys to make
them gallop through the mountains. Then, as if we had done nothing
wrong, we would then return to the Bedouin tent for some freshly baked
pita, haloumi cheese, and tea, which I can still smell all these years later.

SEEKING A BETTER LIFE

My father always wanted to give his children an opportunity to live
outside Israel. He had an offer to teach at a Jewish school in Chicago.
However, upon inquiring with family visiting Israel from Australia,
they didn't describe Chicago favorably and offered to sponsor my parents and all the children to go to Australia instead.

My father's lifelong dream was coming to fruition. He had saved all
his money to be able to get all of us immigration visas to Australia. He
purchased all our tickets by the sweat of his brow, God bless him. I recall
his excitement in the months just before our departure. There was a lot
of tension and confusion about our life-changing move to Australia.

Despite all the mayhem, he led the vision to give all of us a better
future. He set the expectations, had his goal clearly defined, and
achieved it. This was a huge achievement for my dad.

And so, in April 1967, Dad, Mom, Terry, Rebecca, Sophie, and I
moved to Sydney. There, our lives changed forever.

Chapter 2
GOING DOWN UNDER

AN ACT OF KINDNESS

When our family left Israel en route to Australia, we had a layover in Hong Kong. Arriving in Hong Kong was almost surreal; the lights, the signs, the high-rise buildings, and the restaurants were all overwhelming. Dad had purchased bus vouchers to go to our hotel in the Kowloon part of the island, and while driving there, we passed incredible buildings—at least they appeared that way to us. You need to understand that Terry, Rebecca, Sophie, and I had never eaten in a restaurant or seen a hotel until this moment.

We were all in a kind of a daze for a few days. It was better than Disneyland. I was impressed that my dad splurged to buy a transistor radio. At breakfast, we tried to eat the neatly cone-shaped yellow balls that appeared next to our bread, but quickly spit it out when we discovered that it was butter.

After a few days, we got our transportation vouchers back to the airport. We had a great experience up until one incident. As we were approaching passport control, a Chinese official perusing all of our departure documents told my dad he needed to pay a Hong Kong departure tax of 100 HKD for each passenger. My father was confused because he did not anticipate this expense and he had no additional money. Whatever cash he had, he had used up purchasing gifts and small electronics in Hong Kong over the last few days. The official was uncooperative and said, "Sorry, go over there and talk to them." We did not speak English or Chinese but got a sense of the conversation. My dad, sweating and terrified we were going to miss our flight, was getting extremely upset and nervous, not knowing what to do.

All this time, an older English gentleman wearing a straw hat, with a long white beard and a happy Santa Claus face, was observing the commotion. My father was desperately looking in every pocket and satchel for the money he needed to exit. He quietly asked my dad how much he needed. He opened his wallet and gave my father the HK$600 necessary.

I know my dad had tears in his eye at this kindness from a stranger. He asked the old man for his contact information so that he could repay him. The man assured my dad it was OK, to just go ahead and get on the plane. We all got through customs. As we were running to our gate, my father told us to look out for the old man because he didn't get his address. We did not see the dear and kind old man as we excitedly boarded the plane for the last leg of this very adventurous journey. I will never forget this man's act of kindness and generosity.

I have repeated this story on many occasions in my life. I remember it clear as day. I was twelve years old. I tell the story to illustrate to people that the world is a place of outstanding and decent people.

A NEW BEGINNING

David and Uri picked us up from the Sydney airport in two cars—both with big signs on them reading, DAVID's WORLD OF FASHION. I was very impressed by David's black-and-white Holden sedan. It felt like I had landed in heaven and headed home.

We arrived at our new home on top of a hill, by a small lake, in a suburban town called Hurstville. It was a two-story home sitting on a garage below. It felt like I was in a palace by a lake, with the giant eucalyptus trees, birds and kookaburras making the most beautiful sounds throughout the day.

After we had settled in for a night, the next morning Mom asked Terry and me to take the garbage out. We took two containers of refuse down the street by a bunch of trees. To our glee, we discovered that the city arranged garbage trucks to pick up refuse twice a week. It was almost fantastical to us!

David had arrived five years earlier, and Uri three years earlier than we did. When we arrived in Sydney, they both had worked to develop a ladies' clothing retail chain of two stores, which two years after our arrival had expanded to five stores in the suburbs of Sydney.

The entire family was all very excited about the growing family business. We all participated one way or another in all the openings of the stores. David was CEO. My dad worked in the stockroom, while Terry and Uri were working in the stores while distributing and delivering merchandise to the individual shops. Sue and Rebecca managed different stores. After school, I was the "marketing guy" handing out flyers and inviting customers into our stores using a microphone. Sophie was the youngest, so she was kept busy going to elementary school.

THE SMALL FAMILY

David and Uri invited several of the manufacturers who supplied David's World of Fashion merchandise to our home for our first of what would prove to be many Shabbat dinners and lunches. These were memorable get-togethers with lots of great stories about where we all came from. Of course, these dinners featured the most delicious food ever, lots of Hebrew folk singing, and lots of joy. On the other side of the world, the Israeli Six-Day War began three months after our arrival in Sydney.

Approximately one month after we arrived in Sydney, David introduced us one Friday night to the Small family, who manufactured a brand that David purchased for his store, Karina Fashions. They fortunately had teenage twin boys my age—Fred and David. Fred and I became close friends and we have maintained our friendship to this day.

Fred Small recalls in clear detail those early days when we were introduced:

I met Efrem and his family together with my parents, siblings, and grandmother for the first time one sunny Sunday at their home in a southern suburb called Hurstville, in 1967.

As a result of this introduction, via Efrem's big brother David and my father Gad, my life was changed forever. Here was a family large in size (five brothers, three sisters) that in my eyes epitomized the traditional Israeli family: rich in love, culture, and laughter.

For me and my brothers, Lenny and David, that first meeting of the Harkham family opened us up to the Israeli world that my father had described, however until that day we had not directly experienced. That fateful day, we discovered the rich hypnotic smell of Efrem's mother, Aziza's, cooking. It captivated our appetite and senses, taking us to a mysterious world far away.

I met Efrem for the first time: handsome, with an incessant radiant smile and thick, black, curly hair to match. Efrem was instantaneously friendly to my brothers and me. On that special day, there was constant laughter coming from the grown-ups in the house as we, the kids, walked along the riverside looking for tadpoles. By the time my parents, Gad and Rina, and my grandmother were about to leave the Harkham house, my twin brother, David, and I were invited to stay overnight. For us, this was heaven on earth! What an invitation!

The next day was a day of discovering Efrem, and him discovering the Small boys. We all went to the Brighton Le Sands public pool, wearing Efrem's brothers' (Uri and Terry) swimming costumes. I can still feel the cold water of the public pool and that hot Australian summer sun. Mrs. Harkham's food continued to amaze us. Together with her nonstop offerings of exotic dishes and love, Mrs. Harkham renamed me that day: "Friendly" instead of "Freddy." This new name was to become my name within the Harkham family and still applies today.

Those two initial days evolved, particularly for me, into a lifelong friendship with Efrem, already spanning five decades.

Efrem lived an hour or so away from the Sydney Eastern Suburbs, so we had poor access geographically to each other, which did not encourage frequent visits. My father, Gad, and I did numerous Australian bush walks and Efrem was always included, which brought the Small family closer to Efrem. It was a fashion on those walks to wear an Arab *kaffiyeh*. Efrem was most embarrassed and uncomfortable and wouldn't think of wearing it.

One day my father received a call from Efrem's dad, Nagi. He had acquired a home that was a five-minute drive from our family house in the Sydney Harbour area of Rose Bay and only a few minutes' walk from our high school.

Now I began to see Efrem at least five times a week. Our friendship flourished, as we shared most classes. Dover Heights High School was a kaleidoscope of nationalities from Aussies to Greeks, Italians, an Egyptian, and a Turk.

When I think back to my childhood, I realize that it is often the people you know from a young age, who remain your strongest allies and your best lifelong friends. For me, my friend Fred Small is one such friend. I still feel as close to him now as I did while growing up in Australia. His family became like a second family to me. I was regularly invited to join the Small family on many Sundays and on public holidays for one- to two-day adventures. We camped and hiked breathtaking sites throughout New South Wales, the Katoomba Mountains, Little Marley, and others.

During the lengthy drives, my focus was the beautiful classical music Gad, the father, would always listen to. Before meeting the Small family, I was not exposed to this kind of music, which I found soothing, magical, and very expressive.

Gad and Reena's painful life story touched me deeply as a teenager. In 1939, Gad, at age twelve, and his older sister were put on a "kinder boat" full of Jewish children headed for Israel from Germany. Gad's dad arranged to transmit a full payment for a boarding school, which they attended for three years, until they were old enough to work in a kibbutz.

At the age of twenty-one, Gad was notified that his parents and younger brother survived the Second World War and were living in Australia. Gad got a visa to Australia and reunited with his family. Unfortunately, Gad's sister did not get to see her parents again. She was accidentally killed while plowing the tractor on the kibbutz.

I was also privileged to know Reena's mom, Mrs. Royale. She was an angelic and royal woman, who always smiled and radiated positive energy.

During World War II, while being interrogated by the Nazis, Ms. Royale falsified her age—making herself five years younger. Otherwise she would've been separated from her three daughters and deemed old and unproductive to the Nazis.

Reena did not like to discuss the horrors of the camp. But she did say that her mom was extremely protective the entire five years in Auschwitz. She did everything humanly possible to stay united with her three daughters. She never took her eyes off her children the entire time. It was rare and unheard of, that a mother and three daughters could survive Auschwitz as a unit. After the war, Mrs. Royale and her three daughters got a visa to join other family members in Sydney.

I loved being around Mrs. Royale and Reena. I felt their warmth and constant radiating smiles. They were always exuding happiness, despite the pain they endured.

When I mentioned my awe of their positive attitude to Gad, his response was automatic. "It's not okay to inflict our bad moods, burdens and pain on others. We must put happiness into the world—no matter what we are personally going through. It's not okay to reflect our bad moods and pain on to anyone." This had been a valuable life-changing lesson which I constantly recall, especially when I listen to classical music.

A JOYFUL HOME

Three years later, we moved out of the non-Jewish suburb of Hurstville and moved into a beautiful home an hour and a half away on Blake Street in Rose Bay in the Eastern suburbs, where a majority of Jews lived. We loved our new home, which had three more bedrooms and bathrooms than the Hurstville house. We loved being closer to the Pacific Ocean and the Jewish environment. I was now fifteen years old and registered at a public school up the street from our home on Blake Street, Dover Heights Boys High.

The David's World of Fashion franchise count was up to twelve stores at this time. My brother, Ben, was accepted to Sydney Law School, and he also helped David open more stores, after just completing his two-year compulsory duty for the Israeli Defense Forces. The house was full: all five brothers, Rebecca, Sophie, and my parents all lived there. The energy was palpable, fantastic, empowering, enriching, fun. It was like a sleep-away camp with your favorite people in the world.

There was a lot of singing in the showers, especially the older brothers, and delicious aromas of my mother's endless exotic delicacies—in particular the omelets with spinach, onion, tomato, halloumi, and goat cheeses dipped in light tea. Feasts would often continue the entire day, until the major Shabbat event. There was a lot of joy in the Harkham household in those days.

A FOREIGNER IN A FOREIGN LAND

The joy of being in Australia began to dissipate when reality hit and I was enrolled into ninth grade at the local public school, Hurstville Boys High. I arranged to purchase my first school uniform, including a school tie and blazer, which seemed odd to me.

Teenage Australian boys were not accustomed to meeting a foreigner, especially a Jew from Israel. They thought that I, and my Jewish brethren, had a hand in killing their beloved Jesus. The fact that I couldn't speak English did not help the situation. Because of this, the school's local bully group saw a great opportunity in poking fun at me. I was also the subject of constant group gang-ups. I attempted to assert myself to no avail. I was basically a quiet, shy, and introverted teenager, just wanting to get through the school day. Being the youngest boy in the family, I was passive and getting a little chubby from all the good food in our new home. I was too proud to advise any of my family members that I was being teased, ridiculed, and physically abused at school on a daily basis. Unfortunately, the teachers also had no idea of what I was going through.

After a year of this, which felt like a very long time to endure this treatment, I convinced my dad to investigate the likelihood of me going to a Jewish day school—Moriah College—approximately a one-hour commute from Hurstville. After my tests and my dad's final interview with the principal (Mr. Nagle), I received the bad news from my dad—the school had rejected my application. So, I was forced to endure Hurstville Boys High for another two years. Because of this I was forced to develop a hard outer shell that few could penetrate.

I was also too proud to tell my good friend, Fred, that I was being regularly abused at school, fearing I would seem like a cowardly weakling.

Again, I thank God for giving me Shabbat and the Jewish holidays to regain emotional strength and a touch of humanity, as it was a time and a place where I could allow my voice to belt out and sing traditional Hebrew songs with the entire family. At every Shabbat meal, we are obligated to share traditional teachings from the Torah, or its interpretation by its sages. My elder brothers competed to deliver the most captivating story or the Torah's life lessons and its endless wisdom. We call this Shabbat experience "Oneg Shabbat," the Joy of Shabbat. "Oneg" is regularly repeated in the religion to be the highest form of worship.

THE TUNNEL

I am embarrassed to say, despite our family moving to a more Jewish community and having Fred and David Small as friends, I was still a target for the rougher element of the new school. Bullies seem to have extrasensory smell for those kids that feel vulnerable. I was not like the other teenagers and I had no desire to be anything like them. My life experience up to this stage had been far from ordinary.

The rougher element I attracted misinterpreted my introverted personality and quiet demeanor to mean that I looked down on the others, and that I was a snob. The way I coped with this unpleasant part of my youth was to swallow all my anger and fear. It became so overwhelming that I split myself off from my feelings. I disassociated myself from the whole bundle of pain.

During these teenage years, I just wanted to be a better person, and learn as much as I could. I had a thirst for knowledge. I wanted to read only nonfiction books. It was important for me to know the status of the Israeli-Arab conflict. I loved listening to talk radio to get a wider perspective on world affairs. Alistair Cooke, the English BBC Radio commentator, was my absolute favorite for several years. In addition to all this outside information, I was eager to hear words of wisdom and life-changing ideas from my dad, older brothers, and guests that would visit us for Shabbat, especially when we discussed the Torah reading for that particular week. On Sunday afternoon to early evening, the fear and anxiety of being beaten or made fun of would start building. I would begin bracing myself for the conclusion of the peaceful weekend and getting myself ready to be back to the bully battlegrounds. There was no doubt the ruffians sensed my fear when they spotted me at Monday morning assembly and would head my way. My least favorite "gang-up-on-me" was what they referred to as "The Tunnel."

The bullies would take benches and put them across from each other. They would sit close to each other, knees touching each other from across the bench, one rough and mean teenager after another. Then they would throw me in, and I had to get through the very narrow passage of seated kids. They would push me through, and one person after another would punch and hit me until I got out at the other side.

I was thrown into the "The Tunnel" on several occasions and emerged beaten and black-eyed a couple of times. It was not easy to escape from it. Although Fred was not a foreigner, he was also thrown into the "The Tunnel" because he attempted to defend me and other foreign kids. This went on for years at school. Daily, there were all sorts of brutal bullying that I and other foreign kids had to put up with.

I still did not tell my brothers or any family member what was going on, as I was too embarrassed by this. My family would regularly ask me what had happened.

"Why do you have a black eye, Efrem?"

"Efrem, why is your arm broken?"

I would say, "I fell playing sports," or "I tripped and fell." I regularly had black eyes during those teenage school years. Physically it was pretty bad, but emotionally it was even worse.

The teachers were not visible—they were nowhere to be seen on the playground. On one occasion, while minding my own business in a metalwork class, a fellow student slashed my chin with a sharp piece of metal. On this occasion I fought back.

Both of us got expelled from school for two days. My father had to bring me in for a meeting with the principal; otherwise the school wouldn't take me back again. It was a humiliating mess the first time my dad visited my school. Instead of standing up for me, my father assumed I was to blame for the fight.

My father said to me, "I tell you, when are you going to learn? When you associate with idiots, you have to act like an idiot just to get along! You have to go with the flow." I still have the scar on my face from that incident. I was fifteen years old at the time. I remember thinking, "No, I am not going to 'go with the flow.' I am not going to follow the herd mentality."

Finally, the day came for the final confrontation. All the bullying ended after this day, the day I just "lost it." The captain of our rugby team, a strong, burly, and angry guy, kept nagging me and kneeing me every time he saw me. It happened every time he laid eyes on me, and I absolutely dreaded it.

On this particular day, he did something to me that was the last straw in this succession of daily torture. He elbowed me in the back, and that was it! This time, instead of taking the pain, I turned around and knocked him down to the concrete floor. I beat his head onto the ground, all while crying with sounds of deep rage.

I was beating on and screaming at this big hulking bully and acting like a true madman. I felt like I wanted to kill him. Students tried to separate us, and I just would not let this guy go. The onlooking bullies thought that I became insane, and this incident instantly ended the cycle of teenage torture. After that, these bullies were not interested in messing with me anymore. I took all my years of frustration, embarrassment, and fury on this boy and from then on, I felt so much more powerful than I ever had before. From this incredible experience I was able to find my voice, and I was never going to let anyone bully me again.

When we moved "down under," it seemed like I didn't have a single friend in the world. Being an Israeli in this new world of Australia, I was "a stranger in a strange land." That was before I met Fred. As my confidante and a friend for life, he recalls better than I do some of the ordeals we went through at Dover Heights Boys High:

> Because Efrem was obviously not from Australia, the Aussie kids were not especially kind to him, to say the least, testing Efrem's strength in both character and physical fortitude.
>
> Efrem's first few months went from one fight to another, never instigated by Efrem. Efrem's big brother, David, taught him well how to fight back, and it worked. Teachers did not show a great degree of empathy towards Efrem, considering that his broken English limited his ability to communicate in most classes. However, Efrem's determination made up for this temporary disadvantage.
>
> As we all reached our puberty, the interest in girls also took place. Attending dances on a Saturday night became a weekly distraction to our studies. Every Monday was a lively discussion

about who was the first, or the last, to experience, or not experience, a new sexual achievement with the latest new girlfriend. We would describe in detail how far the girls let us go, until they said: "STOP!" Our conquests!

Efrem was always incredibly aware of his obligations to be successful scholastically, incessantly discussing an academic career as a lawyer like his brother, Ben. Efrem's ambitious hunger for financial gain was already obvious. He hid his general competitive traits. In class, we would regularly discuss the family retail fashion business and our post-high school aspirations.

Sports at school were also a challenge for Efrem, as he decided to try out for one of the school's rugby teams, initially having no idea what this game was all about. On the other hand, he was an excellent long-distance runner, always in the top percentile at school.

Sports, to some extent, helped Efrem integrate into the school social network. The kids at school did not appreciate Efrem's assets. Typical boys at that time were not emotionally expressive, sensitive, and forthright; all those attributes that were obviously Efrem's.

Efrem even tried acting in Shakespeare's play, *Macbeth*, at school. His passionate approach was a good fit for this role; however, our drama teacher was not so supportive of Efrem because of his foreign accent.

Numerous peers at school also considered Efrem's giving nature, loyalty, and impeccable integrity as weaknesses. Again, today all the above are Efrem's greatest attributes.

There was one individual that picked an unprovoked fight with Efrem, slicing Efrem's face with a hidden metal piece. Efrem was taken to the hospital and needed stitches. Again, the teachers did not award true justice to the real perpetrator, and rather scolded

Efrem, who was the victim. For the record, Efrem gave this guy a good lesson, and he never touched my mate, Efrem, again. I will never forget that day of the fight. I had cried when I heard what had happened to Efrem, as I felt guilty that I was not there to take revenge on this scoundrel whom, through nothing but jealousy, had attempted to hurt my friend. I had always kept an extra eye out for Efrem at school, but he was more than capable of protecting himself.

Visiting Efrem's wonderful, huge family for Friday night Kiddush dinner continued to be my personal highlight. The love and food of Efrem's mother Aziza, oozed from the Harkham family home in Rose Bay. Laughter, Jewish philosophy, Bible quotes, and world politics were part of the passion of the Harkham Friday nights. Efrem had the highest respect for his parents. He was always a dutiful and loving son to his parents.

Efrem grew into a strong handsome adult, robust in his view of literally everything, and steadfast and unwavering as a Jew, a Zionist, and a proud new Australian. I still remember swimming with Efrem and friends at a Sydney Harbour pool. A stranger came up to Efrem and said, 'I love your curls!' Efrem, by now, had a thick Afro. You could not wipe the smile off Efrem's face.

ANTI-HERD INSTINCT

My father created a clear-cut boundary regarding Shabbat: "You don't leave the house on Friday night." No ifs, ands, or buts. I am thankful that he clearly defined this rule. My siblings and I simply knew that it wasn't an option, and accepted this command, which ended up being one of the most pleasurable memories of my youth.

After school on Friday afternoons, several of our teachers would hang out with their students at a favorite watering hole pub in beautiful Watson Bay overlooking Sydney Harbour, downing schooners of beer and smoking. Thankfully, I never went along. I did not want to go with the herd mentality. I've made an effort to teach my children that it's OK to depart from the herd in order for them to develop their own character and grow as individuals.

I had this fear that if I went out with my peers after school or on the weekend, that I would become lazy, and that I would lose my ambition (and I believe beer gives you a beer gut, which I still don't aspire to develop). My personal drive made certain that I didn't waste my teenage years having fun. In fact, I avoided it because I did not want anything to distract me from my personal goals (I was the same way during my twenties, as well). I felt like I had a big life task ahead and I needed to stay focused to reach it. I realized those years were vital years to prove myself to all those around me that did not believe in me.

I felt that my high school teachers had given up on me and didn't think I had any potential in the world. As far as my education goes, it was in the toilet because I was constantly in fear of my next embarrassment in class and on the playground. I was quiet, withdrawn, and always on guard to ensure I didn't get into a situation that made me a focus of someone's jokes.

At this time, my brother Uri had just ended a relationship with a nice local Jewish teacher—Karen. I found Karen's contact information and arranged for her to be my private tutor. My dad willingly paid for my sessions in my last years in high school. This helped keep my head above water in my academic pursuit. Karen in Hebrew means "ray of light." That is exactly what she was for me—a person who did not allow me to *not* believe in myself. She believed in my abilities, reassuring me of my intelligence and that I was going to do well in my life.

I wanted to start building a life that would sustain a family, and for that it was imperative to create cash flow and financial stability. That drive became my life focus. For me it was worthwhile breaking from the "herd mentality" and focusing whatever energy I had to learn and help my parents financially.

Despite my dismal performance in my final high school exams, I finagled my way into a part-time Sydney University Law School course. I completed three years of law school and was sure that a law degree would help me become more successful. After all, my brother Ben had just completed his five years at Sydney University and was now a lawyer.

THE FAMILY AND THE FASHION BUSINESS

As mentioned earlier, my oldest brother, David, owned two clothing stores when the majority of us arrived in Sydney. My dad had managed to get David out of Israel on his seventeenth birthday. With the little cash my dad gave David upon his departure from Israel, he purchased a Mini Cooper type of van. He acquired merchandise on consignment from local Jewish manufacturers who really loved him, like Gad and Reena Small, and wanted to help him start his business. He loaded up the Mini Cooper with ladies' fashion and went door to door, selling clothes from his car. After three years, he opened his first store, which was so successful that it very quickly grew to become a chain of stores. When he had ten or twelve stores, it became my job to go to the least successful stores, the ones that were not selling enough. I was the marketing guy. I would stand in crowded locations like local train stations and hand out flyers, while wearing a sandwich board promoting David's stores. I also had a mobile microphone. I would holler to crowds of potential patrons: "Welcome to David's World of Fashion! Check out the array of beautiful fashions at incredible prices: Pants $5.99. Sun Frocks $9.99. Shirts from $8.00." Other retailers in the mall hated my hollering.

Between the ages of fifteen and sixteen, I did multiple jobs for David. That is why I always felt natural in the fashion industry. It was a crash course for all of us. I observed what was selling in the stores and I was able to identify what colors and fashion styles women were attracted to try on and hopefully purchase.

I would join my older brother to deliver merchandise to another city in Australia. On this monthly journey, we saw an oak tree that we were impressed by. It had a sign at the bottom of the tree that said, WHILE I LIVE, I WILL GROW. We must always be growing and learning. The department store owner who planted this tree, Anthony Horden, was quoted as saying, "If this tree is to be lasting, it must lay bases for eternity. If it is to be strong, it must have room to grow. It must have earth for its roots and heaven for its branches." That is how I felt in those years. I was always growing and learning. The next few years set the foundation for both my roots in the fashion industry and the unlimited potential to allow my branches to grow.

David's World of Fashion was paying me for the hours I worked at the stores, but I would always give my money to my parents. I clearly recall Mom's numerous requests for more money to maintain the household. Unfortunately, this would set my dad off every time. I found that 95 percent of my parents' battles were about money. As my dad was working for David at the warehouse, things were going from bad to worse at the stores. My dad, like Terry, was deferring receiving a paycheck to help the company survive. When David began to experience financial difficulties, it caused some new problems. That is when the breach happened, and the family stopped working with each other.

My brother Terry was probably David's most devoted employee, but one day he finally decided that he would break away from David's World of Fashion. One of Terry's many tasks in the company was to select merchandise and have them delivered to all of David's stores, all while assisting in supervising the openings of new stores. After years of David's financial difficulties and accepting deferred pay, Terry has only recently broken his silence as to why he decided to leave David's retail company. As he recalls this story, he calls it: "The Eight Cents That Broke My Back."

One very hot summer day in December, Terry had five cents on him, and he felt like having an ice cream. He went into a delicatessen shop next to the company headquarters and requested an ice cream. The lady who waited on him said, "That will be eight cents."

Terry said, "I am three cents short," hoping the lady would overlook the difference. She did not.

This incident hit home for Terry that he needed to make some changes in his life. When he walked into David's World of Fashion headquarters, he saw a new attendant in the reception area. She was a beautiful blue-eyed, blonde girl. "What the hell? Where did you come from? David just hired another new secretary? Is David here? Where is he?" Terry demanded to know.

"David is in a meeting," the new receptionist replied.

"I want to talk to him," Terry said.

"He is in a meeting," she argued.

So Terry waited for a few minutes. When the manager finally came out, David emerged from the office. Terry started right in on him.

"David, you hired another employee? You owe me several months' salary. I want to help your company, but I can't go on living like this." So, he gave David an ultimatum: "Is it going to be me, or the girl? One of us has to go."

David said to Terry, "She's staying, and if you don't like it, the door is right there."

And so, Terry was now finished with David's World of Fashion. Seven months earlier, Terry had met a Canadian Jewish family traveling through Sydney who were our guests for a Friday night Shabbat dinner. He connected with them in Toronto and said he was planning to get more fashion work experience abroad. They welcomed him to their home and also introduced him to close friends who owned fashion department stores throughout Canada. This experience was extremely valuable to Terry. He left and worked with them for approximately eighteen months before returning home.

When Terry returned to Sydney, he started his own women's apparel company in Sydney called Lulu Fashions, named after my dad's mother's name in Arabic, meaning "pearls."

At the time, I was eighteen years old and had just begun attending an evening course at the University of Sydney Law School. The university was in the heart of Sydney and located only a fifteen-minute walk from Terry's new factory for Lulu Fashions. During the day, I worked for a law firm in the city as an articles clerk, getting practical legal experience during the day while studying law at night.

OPPORTUNITY KNOCKS

One day I went to visit Terry. As I opened the door to his new factory, I saw Terry standing at the end of the factory floor, with no other employees around. He seemed extremely disheartened, and had his arms folded in resignation. He told me he was having a very difficult time getting his new business off the ground. I asked to see his collection of five or six dress and blouse samples. They looked dowdy and boring.

I said to him, "Terry, let me help you, please. Give me your fashion samples and I'll show them around and hopefully get orders from retailers in the city."

He was hopeful and thankful that I had offered to assist him in the sales department. This became my new crusade. I was ready to run. I had a clear goal, purpose, and mission. The "why" behind it was easy: I had an opportunity to assist a dear and kind brother who was suffering with his new business. After all, I was thankful to Terry because he always was there for me as an older brother. He always included me in all of his activities in Zikhron, Petah Tikva, and Sydney, never being embarrassed by the younger brother tagging along.

The fact that I had no knowledge or experience selling the collection to retailers didn't deter my commitment to assist Terry. The timing was critical, and I had to do this ASAP, or he might have to close his new enterprise.

After several weeks meeting with numerous retailers, I realized that there was an opportunity in salvaging Terry's company. Though I enjoyed my time there, I approached the law firm I had worked at for just over a year and asked to be released from my obligation. I was pleasantly surprised at how my colleagues in the small law firm were disappointed to see my departure. However, I maintained my commitment to the law school four nights a week.

I had an exit interview and I met with the owner of the law firm, Roderick B. Harris. I mustered the confidence to ask why he hired me, when I knew there were other law students that were more qualified seeking the same job. His response had a profound effect on me. He said, "When I interviewed you, you look like you had *nous*." I asked him what that word meant, and he said, "*Nous* is when you have common sense and practical intelligence. I could see that you had a special drive and that nothing would stand in your way to get anything done." Coming from the owner of the law firm, it gave me a lot of confidence. I still refer to this word in describing anyone that I find to have this level of tenacity, derived from using common sense.

I became a traveling salesman, going from city to city, meeting new retailers and showing Terry's samples, hoping to get orders for the collection. Their reaction was usually some variation of "your collection is very nice, but I don't think it's going to sell for us."

I was always genuinely appreciative for the time they allotted to see "the line." I would even return several weeks later with corrections, changes, or additions to the collection.

I began to develop a relationship with the retailers. They seemed to feel sympathy for me and appreciated my effort driving out to meet them. The clients I visited regularly began to give me genuine input about how the line should look, and actually gave me samples of items that were selling very well, for us to copy. This was a huge break-through for the company.

Our patternmaker, Mrs. Zalinka, would take the proven sellers apart at the seams and trace the contours of the dress top or jumpsuit and make a pattern. We would purchase identical or better fabrics, trace the new patterns onto it, and sew them together. Our final sample turned out identical or even better than the original with better quality and at a lower price, due to our extremely trim overhead expenses.

We were now convinced we were onto something. Our collection was looking fresh, colorful, and well made. The initial orders we fulfilled were sold out every time. This gave me the confidence to visit and sell more retailers, because I was now certain that I was proposing a win/win situation. I was sure that the retailers who purchased our product would sell through very well.

I overcame my insecurity and fear of "cold-calling" new prospective buyers. Whenever I returned to present a collection to a customer, I made certain my presentations and the look of the samples were improving and reinforced my selling skills.

Up until this time, I was driving a four-door 1965 Mazda station wagon that I purchased for $165 after I got my license. The reason I got such a great deal on the Mazda was that it had some serious deficiencies. Its biggest issue was the car didn't go into reverse gear, so I had to be creative about where I could park. Another was that it was missing windshield wipers. In order to see when it rained, I carried a batch of potatoes that I would cut and smear on the front of the windshield so the raindrops would slide off smoothly. The driver's window also had a stick to prop it up in order to keep it closed. There was no way I could roll the window down.

In spite of these problems, I was extremely thankful to have a car. Once we were doing well enough, I began looking for other car options. We decided to buy a fancy vintage four-door sedan owned by our local gas station proprietor one block from our factory. After a few months, we also purchased a brand-new Toyota Celica hatchback, which was like a driving dream.

I realized, in order to sell successfully, I needed to develop and demonstrate absolute self-confidence. This was not easy for me to do. I selected several role models that I would emulate. One was my older brother, David. I would constantly wear David's suits and ties for all my sales calls. I didn't just borrow David's suits; I borrowed his charming smile and personality. Having four older brothers provided me a large selection of clothes I could borrow to assist me to look older, established, and successful so that the buyers would be comfortable to order our merchandise.

I looked everywhere for examples of self-confidence. I would regularly listen to BBC radio commentator and novelist Alastair Cooke. I loved his warm and intelligent, comforting voice. I listened over and over again to recordings of John F. Kennedy's speeches. I read and reread Dale Carnegie's *How to Win Friends and Influence People* almost nightly. I was determined to create a new self, a new identity, so I utilized various self-improvement tapes and books.

I enjoyed the weekly TV series *The Fugitive* starring David Janssen. I wanted to emulate his integrity, though he had a beaten-down, almost serious, yet honest look.

At this time, I began making a list of the top thirty most desirable accounts in Sydney. I was determined every single day to focus on developing a dialogue and ultimately a relationship with these desirable accounts. Several years ago, my brother Terry brought me a compilation of the calendars and lists I used to make in those early years as a souvenir of my intense work ethic.

I set goals daily. I needed to get several orders every single day in order not to feel like a failure. I continue to make my list on a daily basis to ensure I keep moving forward in my business and personal life. I also learned that every successful sale is the result of multiple meetings.

I quickly developed a four-step guide that I put into practice at almost every single meeting and inserted into presentations that I made. I realized it was imperative that my buyer felt that I was a genuine and caring listener. I was also determined to draw out and develop a personal connection with the buyers. My method included:

- Listen: I would listen to the clients and show I was paying attention. I would respond with an "Ahhhhah" after they would make a specific point.
- Acknowledge: I would say "I understand." This would reassure them that I was on the same thought process to show we were in agreement.
- Elaborate: If there was a subject a buyer seemed interested to discuss, I'd say, "Can you tell me more about that?" which always created a longer dialogue.
- Repeat: I would finally repeat the gist of the conversation. I would say "what I hear you saying is . . ."

I would present the product I wanted to sell if it was appropriate to do at that point of contact in the relationship. This method helped me connect and foster long-term relationships with many of my accounts.

I still repeat this guide for listening to my team approximately forty years after I initially used it as a process to connect with people. By just listening, I found I could usually identify how I could establish a beneficial business relationship with a person.

For me, relationships happen only when there's a face-to-face connection. But first we must listen to the other person's story and how they got to this juncture in their life to grow an initial connection.

I had lots of practice and felt safer listening from a very young age. This capacity to be comfortable with my silence was especially imprinted during my high school days in Sydney. Besides, to me, everyone else's story and opinions fascinated me more than my own. I am always interested in learning about the life of another, especially my guests, whether at the hotels or in my home. My story is way too long and complicated and I always prefer hearing about their journey more than discussing mine. Having this trait in my personality always drew people out. I believe this gave me an edge over my competition. It also added a personal touch and authenticity to most of my encounters with my various buyers, team members, children, and friends.

QUALITY CONTROL

From my early sales and marketing experience at Lulu, I learned that my word was my bond and that we had to honor our promises. At almost every presentation, I assured the prospective buyer of our guarantee of excellent quality for all the merchandise we shipped. I also promised that goods ordered would be delivered as specified on the order, or earlier. These two points were always "the elephant in the room" that I needed to discuss every time. In hindsight, offering this guarantee of perfect fitting garments, quality sewing, and trimming of threads put us way ahead of our competition. Within a year, our prices were in line with our established competitors.

Terry approached me several months into the relationship and offered me a 50 percent partnership in Lulu Fashions. My immediate response was, "Are you sure you know what you are offering me?"

And I continued to say, "I don't think you realize how much potential this company has."

He responded, "That's why I want you to be my partner."

Of course, I was jubilant at this very generous offer and I accepted.

This first partnership with Terry taught me that in order for a business relationship to thrive, we had to be willing to confront and challenge each other's ideas and plans without any constraints. Terry's consistent expression of gratitude for my contribution to the entire operation was extremely powerful. He has often spoken to me of the blessings I brought to his life since I started working with him. I feel blessed as well, since he definitely put the wind in my sail, which I badly needed.

To my surprise in the partnership, Terry took and applied 98 percent of my ideas, suggestions, and requests. We had a different way of doing business. Terry was more involved in the production side of the business, and being the frugal older brother, he would attempt to substitute fabrics that had a similar look and feel to the original sample but were less costly. Yet, in the end, we always ended up doing the right thing for our clients. He understood my obsessive need to give the customer exactly what they ordered, including not compromising the quality of fabrics and striving to deliver a perfect garment, every time, irrespective of how much we sold it for.

From the beginning, I aspired to be the best businessperson I could be. Being thought of as the second best or mediocre in this, my first enterprise, was absolutely not in the books for me. I had the polar opposite mentality of doing the "bare minimum" of what was expected.

There were numerous days that Terry, along with the crew and me at Lulu, worked around the clock to ensure that we honored our commitment to deliver our product on time. I recall my dialogue with the sewers, reminding them to truly care about the workmanship of our production. Every garment was checked top to bottom to ensure it was up to the standard expected by the client before they left our warehouse.

PERSISTENCE PAYS OFF

Then, I had the good fortune of meeting with Joan Giles. She was an older lady, and a true-blue Aussie.

My meeting with Joan Giles was a life lesson for the power of perseverance. Joan was an important buyer in Sydney for a company called Rockmans, which was a higher-end division of Woolworth's Department Stores. On the first Tuesday of every month, she had an "open door" policy for suppliers who sat in the corporate waiting room, each eager to have a few minutes in her presence, trying to sell her their line of clothes for her six hundred stores.

It took me six visits to her monthly "open door" policy to actually make a connection with Joan. I was determined not to let this potential sale slip away, no matter how many "open door" Tuesdays I had to stake myself in her waiting room.

Finally, on the seventh visit, the week of my twentieth birthday, I realized I needed to get her attention, which I had not done in the previous six visits. It was my turn to present my collection. I walked into her office, took a seat, and did not speak, waiting for her to raise her eyes from her computer reports she was perusing.

She said, "What are you waiting for?"

I said, "I've been coming here for the last six months. I work for a ladies' fashion house called Lulu."

"Where are your samples?" she said, making me feel like an idiot.

"They are in my car, in your parking lot downstairs." I explained sheepishly. "I have shown them to you for the last six months."

She asked "Well, do you want to show them to me again?"

I replied, "Absolutely."

"Well, run along and go and get them."

"Yes ma'am," I said as I scurried off to my car and returned with the samples. She took one look at the collection and asked about our quality, which I assured her was excellent. I insisted that the jumpsuit was magical, a proven seller, and that many stores that tried it ended up reordering it.

In those early days, a sale rarely happened instantaneously. It had taken me seven contacts to get Joan's sale. That's the lucky number. Seven contacts spelled success! This led me to my favorite mantra, "Every Sale Is a Result of Multiple Sales"—for every sale you make, you have to sell yourself and/or your product a few times prior for the final sale to be made.

That particular Tuesday, Joan decided to give us a try and ordered twelve pieces of style #45, a gabardine jumpsuit, for one store. The next day she called me and advised me that she had sold seven of the twelve and she placed another order for thirty-six pieces to supply to three stores. The jumpsuits we were delivering kept selling. Orders came from her for 120, then for 240, and then thousands upon thousands for her six hundred stores throughout Australia. She ordered three styles for all six hundred of her stores and kept reordering the items over and over again because of their incredible sell-throughs. Joan Giles put us in every one of her stores and literally put our company on the map.

At her company's expense, Joanne began buying several two-page spreads advertising our products in national newspapers, such as the *Daily Mirror*. Across the two-page ad would read: "RAZZLE DAZZLE with LULU FASHIONS AT ROCKMANS." She would have sketches of the outfits she purchased from us stretch from one page to the next.

Our product was displayed in windows in all Rockmans stores. We began to receive hundreds of calls from other retailers, asking to make an appointment to review our collection and place orders.

Joan's competitors at every one of the six hundred stores had suddenly learned about the Lulu brand, and they all wanted to purchase our fashion collection as well. Before long, I didn't have to go from store to store trying to sell our line of clothing. Stores and department store chains were now seeking us out.

I was amazed. In only ten to twelve months our showroom went from feeling like a ghost town, to the point where it felt like a bustling train station of activity. There were people coming into the factory, taking merchandise with them, and placing additional orders for other styles. It was an incredibly exhilarating experience.

I had never seen so many checks and cash pouring in. Terry and I had never been exposed to this kind of success in our lives! It was beyond our wildest dreams, an amazing accomplishment, and no one was more astonished than me!

Lulu went on to become a significant manufacturer of ladies' clothing in Australia. Since Terry and I were then equal partners in the success of Lulu, I was able to personally make a million dollars for myself by the age of twenty-one.

Joan Giles became a good friend. She even later came to visit me and was my houseguest in Beverly Hills. I will always be grateful for the most important lessons that Joan taught me that I still use in my daily business interactions. The most important lesson that I teach my sales team is not to give up.

I was still determined to stay the course and complete my law studies. With my full-time job at Lulu Fashions, I had little time for anything else. I stayed with my law studies when I later moved to the US and did so by correspondence classes. I was into my third year of studying law. Finally, I decided to abandon it altogether for the very demanding job in the garment business.

It was amazing to me that with no formal business education, there I was in the middle of running a very successful garment company, in the growing economy of the late 1970s.

I quickly learned that in order to succeed in the business world, I must have a clear objective and decide what I want in life. I started out with two BIG goals. I wanted to assist my parents with financial support. I also needed to prove to the people around me, particularly my former teachers and bullies, that I was going to succeed.

It's the same drive that compels me today. When I see the potential of any project or enterprise, I jump at the opportunity. I am propelled by the potential.

The fact that I overcame my insecurity and lack of knowledge of the business should be an inspiration for others and is one of the main reasons I wrote this book. It was not until a lot later when I was financially successful that I was able to free myself from this lack of self-confidence and became the Efrem Harkham I was meant to be. If I can do it, I believe that others are able to do it as well.

WHEN ONE DOOR CLOSES, ANOTHER ONE OPENS

When I was twenty-one, Terry and I invited a third brother, Ben, to join us as at Lulu. Ben was in Los Angeles at the time, trying his hand at manufacturing ladies' fashion. He returned to Australia, at our invitation, to partner with us. Ben was the law graduate who focused on creating a sustainable infrastructure with the processes and systems for our rapidly growing fashion business. He was driven and very smart. He was always focused on the company's financials and constantly pursued data for the numbers that really mattered to the success of the business. We were thriving and the company was very successful. We added to our force a reputable sales rep in Melbourne, David Wise, which also helped us continue to grow. We were dispatching tens of thousands of shorts, blouses, jumpsuits, and dresses to almost every city in Australia. People were coming out of the woodwork from markets that I did not know existed.

I will never forget one late summer afternoon. Ben, Terry, and I were in a meeting in our newly built and beautifully outfitted showroom inside the factory. A frantic, well-dressed, and fully made-up drag queen named Tom had driven four hours from a small town in southern Australia called Toowoomba. In the past we had sold to Tom merchandise over the phone but never met him in person. We were so excited to have clients from all walks of life and were delighted to hear his gratitude for our commitment to producing well-made, affordable clothing that was "selling like hotcakes" in his store. Like all the other clients, he placed orders on our upcoming collection, and he selected merchandise off our racks and loaded them into his wagon. At the end of the day, it was our clients, the service we gave them, and the high-quality product we sold to them that brought us success.

Despite our success, I didn't feel adequate. I stopped living my theory: In order for any relationship or partnership to succeed, the individuals need to confront and challenge issues and concerns as they were happening, without delay. There were issues that I should have confronted with my brothers and our working relationship, but instead I kept it all inside. This built a rage inside of me that I was not able to cope with. I began to constantly lose my temper and I became increasingly bitter. I started to drive erratically, smoking almost a pack of cigarettes a day, which wasn't like me at all. I knew these were signals to get help. I realized I needed to get off my high horse and be humble enough to seek help. I was concerned that my anger and recklessness would result in running someone over.

One day, I pulled into a Crisis Center in Sydney, and I explained to a counselor there that I was afraid I was going to kill someone through my erratic, angry driving.

"Why are you feeling so stressed and in this frame of mind?" he asked me.

I explained my frustration working with Ben and Terry.

"And what do you want to do?"

I said, "I don't know. I love California. I know I could start a business there and build a life for myself."

He said, "Do you know America?"

And I said, "Yeah, I have been to New York and Los Angeles on several occasions to get fashion ideas and inspirations. I go there to see the latest trends. Los Angeles is a lot like Sydney, and I love it."

"Can you afford being in America?" he asked me.

"Yeah, I think I may be a millionaire."

"You *think* you may be a millionaire?!" he said with astonishment. "Then what are you doing here?"

I said, "Because I have a business here."

He asked, "Well, if it is your business, can you sell your share and go to America?"

I thought for a minute, and I said, "Yes."

That counselor really defined the perfect solution to my problems and my frustration. Within a week, I explained to Terry and Ben that I needed to move on and sell my share of Lulu Fashions.

I was sorry to leave behind friends like Fred Small, but I knew I had to leave Australia. I arranged for my departure, bought a plane ticket, and moved to Los Angeles.

Luckily, I was not greedy about determining the value of my share of the Lulu Company. Terry and Ben were very fair. I left Sydney and they honorably wired me a million dollars a short period after my departure, and I set out to start a new life for myself in America.

Chapter 3
HELLO HOLLYWOOD

LAUREL WAY

I came to Los Angeles with two suitcases in tow. I got into a yellow cab at LAX airport and asked to be taken to Sunset Boulevard in West Hollywood, near the Laugh Factory and Greenblatt's Deli. It was probably the longest taxi ride I have ever experienced with so many thoughts streaming through my mind. I was so excited about the next big venture of my life. I recall the feeling of confidence and certainty that I'd make my life better than it had been.

I saw the world exactly as it was in that moment. It took a lot of guts to just board a plane for California, away from my family and friends, and I am glad I was able to suck up all the fears. I just could not wait to start. I knew that it was all going to work out, as it always does.

I dragged my suitcase a few hundred yards from Sunset, up Laurel Avenue to the first apartment building I saw. I rang the manager's buzzer and met a Mrs. May, who was also the owner of the building.

After a short conversation, and using my natural charm, Mrs. May (God bless her), agreed to ignore the fact that I did not have a Social Security number or a US bank account, etc. She was very kind to have made it so easy for me and allow me to move into an apartment that same day. To this day, I am thankful for her act of kindness and trust at that moment.

The morning after my arrival in LA, I met with my dear family friend Harold Wolfson. He was my seventy-year-old American buddy, a non-practicing attorney, and later my real estate broker. At the time I thought he was truly my guardian angel, and he gave me an added sense of confidence, having just arrived in a strange town, not knowing anyone. He made sure I was OK, constantly checking in on me, and I loved that he was always ready to do a favor. He was extremely friendly and easy to be around. I proudly introduced him to my landlady and showed him my apartment building, so he would know where I lived just in case of an emergency.

Harold even lent me a spare old Chevrolet station wagon to use until I was ready to buy a car. The car was not a "girl magnet," to say the least. It had a loud exhaust sound and it guzzled a lot of gas. I recall meeting a girl at the California Mart and when I went to pick her up from her apartment the following evening for a date, she was in a state of shock when she saw Harold's Chevrolet. It was not an enjoyable evening. Needless to say, I did not see her again.

I'm eternally grateful to Harold for assisting me in getting all the necessities, including a US driver's license, a Social Security number, and all the other legal tidbits. Anyone who moves to a strange town should have a "Harold." He made my transition as smooth as possible.

One day, after meeting with Harold, I had him drop me off on Hollywood Boulevard so I could take a four-hour tour of the city. My goal was to become familiar with the area. It was very fun to be a tourist. Across the street from my new apartment on Sunset Boulevard was the legendary Schwab's Pharmacy. That was where many actors would pick up their favorite magazines or accessories and have a seat by the semicircular fountain bar for a drink, dessert, or casual meal. I remember seeing both Ernest Borgnine and Tim Conway—who I had watched regularly on the TV series *McHale's Navy*—Dean Martin, and numerous other movie stars there. I feel fortunate to have experienced a bit of that "old Hollywood" era that began to fade away in the early 1980s.

I was also intrigued by the No Cruising signs that graced the entire length of Sunset Boulevard. I started exploring Sunset on foot, discovering my new environment. I quickly learned that West Hollywood was also known worldwide as "Boys' Town." The number of advances I got from men in that section were way more than from women. Even though I wanted to discover my surroundings, I was afraid to be a voyeur in that world. It seemed exciting because they were a community that lived the life they wanted to live. But I felt it was very risky and was not worth entering the theaters, bars, and clubs that had men and women pouring in and out at all hours of the night.

I was also amazed by how easily and readily available drugs were in restaurants, clubs, and on the street. The big three being offered at the time were cocaine, marijuana, and Quaaludes. I was determined not to experiment, except for the one bachelor party I went to approximately five years after arriving in LA. I had indulged in cocaine that night and I had endless thoughts streaming through my mind. I thought I was going to go crazy. I became more wired than I usually am, which is a scary sight. This was clearly not for me.

Seeing the effect of marijuana on people using it was in itself a turn-off. The image of the extreme zoned-out relaxation and the lazy eyes did not appeal to me either. The sight of Quaalude pills and their scientific name, methaqualone, was scary. My fears kept me from plunging into the world of drugs, which would have been very easy for me in those days because of the access and the fact that for the first time, I was on my own and free to do as I pleased in such an exciting city.

Also, on the boulevards, there were a multitude of erotica stores and escort services for any kind of sensual experience—transgender, male, or female. This was being offered on many street corners on Sunset, Santa Monica, and Hollywood. I walked into a strip club on Sunset called the Seventh Veil. There were pretty women dancing topless around poles, and lots of desperate eyes of men wanting to get close to the women. They were not allowed to touch. The audience was mostly drunk, slurring words of passion to the dancers. Sometimes they would approach a dancer and shower her with lots of dollar bills. The other men in the room looked like they were embarrassed to be seen there. This was a bit of a culture shock for me as I had not experienced anything like it in Australia. The environment was extremely dark and was not for me.

During the first few weeks in LA, I was having lunch at the iconic Tiny Naylor's—a diner on Sunset Boulevard—when two young, attractive Israeli girls at the table next to me began a conversation. They succeeded in encouraging me after lunch to tour the Church of Scientology headquarters with them, which was located a few blocks away.

They were enamored by the organization and were anxious for me to become involved. I was open to socializing and meeting people my age, as well as hopefully finding spiritual guidance.

After the tour, they arranged what they called an "audit" for me. This was an interview with one of the counselors at the church. This was a taped question and answer session. The first thirty minutes was an enjoyable and easy conversation about my background and life story. Then the questions changed to have a more serious tone. The counselor mentioned individuals I discussed in the first thirty minutes. He asked me to talk more in depth about my relationships. I found it difficult to discuss details about those people, especially about my family members, on tape. The counselor explained that Ron Hubbard's theory is that we all have suppressed powers and abilities that we could access on the condition that we deal with the discomfort and scars certain people have caused us. When I asked the counselor for more detail about the techniques of the organization, her response made my "warning antenna" go up.

"We are immortal beings in the physical body." Then she added, "We have all had many past lives on extraterrestrial planets." That afternoon, I determined that Scientology was not for me. This was not where I was going to fill my thirst for wisdom, however attractive the girls were.

I loved my newfound freedom. I experienced an entirely new world that I had no idea existed. I had lived with my family for the last twenty-one years. With the new freedom, I realized I had to make some serious choices and that I was solely responsible for where I ended up.

I needed to exercise my "100 Percent Block Rule" with regards to certain elements prevalent in the late 1970s and early 1980s. I blocked these opportunities "just in case I liked it." I am human after all. Had I let my guard down and acted immaturely, my destiny would no longer be in my control.

To succeed in business, I thought I needed to look good. As a result, I needed to take care of my body and maintain my shape, especially if I was going to be a ladies' fashion manufacturer. I began my three-to-five mile running regimen in those early days in West Los Angeles.

I recall that every time I rejected an alluring offer, I felt that I was in control of my destiny. This kind of self-control was and still is empowering to me. My purpose for coming to LA was to start a business and to make my parents' lives better. I also had to prove to my teachers and to a bunch of bullies in Sydney that I was worthy, and I could make it. I suppose I had a barometer from my parents that did not allow me to do certain things. I'm proud that I was mature and responsible for my well-being. I was able to reap rewards from the decisions I made and from the situations that I did not allow myself to experience, especially in hindsight.

Another reason that ensured I did not pursue the "fun" and playful aspect of my new surroundings was my application to continue, by correspondence, my third year of law school at Sydney University. I decided to study law so that I would not be taken advantage of in business. Pursuing my law education was another way of making me the best person that I could be.

LULU USA

My primary goal at that time was to start my own clothing line. The first step in that endeavor was to find a factory in a suitable location. With Harold Wolfson's assistance, I found a great 5,000-square-foot factory space on South Alameda Street in downtown LA. I signed a one-year lease, with a two-year option.

The next step was to find a talented designer that would take the risk of working with a young start-up that had never manufactured clothing in the US before. At least six designers that I interviewed did not respond to meet for a second interview. Then I interviewed Mary Donovan. I realized God really loved me when Mary walked into the interview. I loved her portfolio of past designs. More importantly, she inquired about my story and was happy to meet for the second and third interviews.

My goal was to create a group of twenty to twenty-five career dresses, blouses, and skirts combinations for the growing career woman sector between the ages of twenty-five to fifty. The look was unfussy and timelessly classical enough that it would flatter women's shapes and different body types. The variety of fabrics we used was also very important to me. They could be plain, printed, or striped with the look and feel of the high-fashion designers like Giorgio Armani, Versace, and Chanel. However, unlike those designer fabrics, I wanted ours to be machine washable.

I wanted to present a line that would look attractive hanging on a hanger, that would speak to the consumer, saying, "Pick me up, try me on." I also expressed the importance of outfitting the dresses in the collection with different belts and accessories to show the different looks that could be shown with our collection.

Finally, I wanted our dresses to sell under $100 at retail. Our consumer had to feel that she was getting a tremendous value for the money she was spending.

Mary saw the vision and loved the direction. However, I had one more big request. I asked her to put aside designs and ideas that she had successfully created and produced in the past and follow my lead, which had proven to be successful in a very short period in Australia. She agreed to my terms and we committed to each other for a minimum of one year. We ended up working together for over ten years.

Over the next two days, Mary and I spent entire days shopping various malls and stores on Rodeo Drive in Beverly Hills, Century City, downtown LA, and Sherman Oaks. We bought over fifty samples of the absolute bestselling career clothes for women. Fortunately, Mary had three employees that followed her wherever she worked—a pattern maker, a sample sewer, and a cutter. We installed three fifty-foot by seventy-two-inch wooden cutting tables, which was the whole length of the factory. We also purchased all the necessary equipment needed to create and produce a great collection of women's clothing. From the beginning of the operation, I was aware that even though I was younger than all four of my employees, it was up to me to create the atmosphere in the factory. If I wanted others to be upbeat and happy, then I had to smile. If I wanted my team to respect me, I had to show my respect for them. We were off and running.

Within three months our team completed the presentation of our first collection of fifteen dresses, under the LULU USA label. The final days before a collection is complete and ready to be shown is an extremely stressful period with lots of emotions, last-minute changes, additions and deletions to the collection. Unfortunately, one of my traits all my years in the fashion business was the pursuit of absolute excellence that resulted in me never completely being satisfied with any of my collections. My issue with this first collection was primarily the fabrics. They did not have the high-fashion quality and classical feel and look that I had envisioned.

Despite my concerns about the shortcoming of the line, it was well received, and orders began to come in. Mary introduced me to a sales rep in the California Mart to sell my first collection in the Western USA. He had other lines in the showroom, but none with the same career focus. We began ordering fabric in bulk to produce the orders. Approximately six weeks later we began shipping our orders, and reorders began to come in.

Six months after landing in LA, my first collection was designed, invoiced, and shipped to stores all over California. There was no turning back. It was time to start working on the second dress collection. It was time to grow our distribution into other states.

NO ONE DRESSES A WOMAN LIKE JONATHAN MARTIN

This seemed like a good time to reconnect with my brother Uri. He had moved to LA from Sydney in the early 1970s. I went over to their house and I apologized to Uri and his wife, Sally, for my being a stranger all these months while I was setting up my business.

Uri and Sally, together with a partner, started a great collection of beautiful women's blouses and shirts called Jonathan Martin. Eventually Uri purchased his partner's 50 percent share of the company and became the sole owner of Jonathan Martin.

My family in Australia began a "work with your brother" campaign. This was done by numerous phone calls from my mother and father telling me about the power of "brotherly love." My older brothers were also encouraging me to work together with Uri, saying that we should combine our energies and join forces. They would ask, "Why do it separately?" and pointed out that Uri was under tremendous pressure from his growing company.

The call that tipped the scale was from my older sister Sue, who was living in Sydney at the time. She was the wise one in the family. She said, "Efrem, you're making dresses, Uri is making blouses. You'll both be so busy working these divisions, you won't even see each other. There is nothing to worry about. Join forces and it's bound to succeed. I am telling you."

Uri and I met on a few occasions at his factory, which was shipping approximately $10 million annually. The opportunity was beginning to gel, despite my commitment not to work with another family member.

During our meeting I was salivating at the site of Uri's massive inventory of beautiful fabrics, neatly stored under the eight eighty-foot-long wooden cutting tables in his 12,000-square-foot factory space on Grand Avenue and 11th Street in downtown LA. Uri was importing elegant couture-type easy-to-care-for materials, primarily from Japan and Milan. All I could see were the dollar signs and how great these fabrics would look in my new Career Dress Collection.

There's approximately ten years difference in age between Uri and me. We did not know each other as adults, as he had been in LA for the prior five years. We did not experience working with each other in the past, but we respected each other. He appreciated my being upfront regarding certain boundaries. One big one for me was that I did not want him to meddle with any part of the dress division—design, production, and shipping. I wanted to solely handle that division, down to the minutest detail.

Uri gladly agreed, because he was unfamiliar with the dress market. However, he pointed out, "I need your help with the shirt division. The quality control needs a serious overhaul." I agreed to take on this responsibility.

There was one other boundary that I set in stone that Uri respected—not to intermingle business into our private lives. Uri's appetite for success was perhaps stronger than mine. He was very ambitious and was driven to succeed the entire time I have known him. I wanted to maintain a balance in my life and set the expectations and I needed to break from the business after hours. I purchased 50 percent of the Jonathan Martin clothing line from Uri for approximately $1 million. We were now partners.

My team at South Alameda was happy to move into the Jonathan Martin factory on 11th Street and Grand Avenue. We were going to be part of a bigger team. I constantly repeated to my team that they reported to no one else but me. It was very empowering for them to know I cared so much for their well-being, and I assured them that I would take care of them.

The Jonathan Martin dress division began to operate instantly. We already had orders to cut, sew, and deliver. The infusion of the dress division was a major jolt to the company's overall performance. All that inventory of fabric sitting under all those cutting tables turned into cash within a very short time. The dress division was a sensation in stores throughout the US.

Uri had a great blouse salesman in New York City, Steven Feinstein. Fashion buyers and people in general were very drawn to Steven. He was a whiz of a salesman. I have always been in awe of people who had the gift of being able to connect with clients on a deeper psychological level. Fortunately, Steve's parents Zack and Lee sold dresses across the street on 38th Street and Broadway. I regarded Zack as the best salesman I had ever met. He and Leona (Lee) were a package deal. They were a great team. They loved the vocal duet of Steve Lawrence and Eydie Gorme, who were also an inseparable husband-and-wife team.

Zack and Lee had a 3,000-square-foot showroom in a predominantly dress-design building. They represented five different dress collections in their showroom. Ours became the sixth. We signed an agreement that they would solely represent the Jonathan Martin dress collection on the East Coast. Approximately sixty days after our meeting in New York, and after our initial deliveries of dresses, the line was selling like hotcakes. The dresses were flying out of the stores. Major chains began ordering the collection and placing huge reorders. We were a hit.

Zack came to meet me in LA, to tell me in person that he and Lee had decided to drop the five other dress collections in their showroom and that, going forward, they would solely represent the Jonathan Martin dress line. This was a milestone day for me.

Zack was around sixty-five years old when we began working together. He was five foot eleven, slim, handsome, and always tanned. He always smiled to make sure we all saw his pearly white teeth shimmer. He always wore beautiful suits and shirts and he had a great choice of fashionable ties. I have a hunch that he blow-dried his hair, and his nails were always very clean with clear polish.

The buyers that came to shop in the showrooms were mostly women of all ages, from a multitude of backgrounds. Zack had an uncanny ability to make everyone that came into his world feel loved and appreciated. I watched him as he offered to take and hang their jackets, always offering them a Diet Coke with ice. Zack had a happy inner being that was always expressed on his face. Within the first few minutes of meeting anyone, old or new acquaintances, he would ask them how life was treating them or how everything was going. He genuinely wanted to know about the well-being of those that came across his path. He would ask about their husbands, wives, girlfriends, and children. After listening to his buyers for a few minutes, he would turn to them and inquire into their business. Somehow, during the conversation, he would always ask about recent vacations, what the buyer was doing for upcoming holidays, and what they had planned for New Year's. After Zack schmoozed with the buyers in his deep Brooklyn accent, Lee would enter the cubicle where they were showing the line and talking. She liked to join, especially if it was a department store or a large account. She would get a quick recap of the conversation and then she would bring out the collection and present it. If they were buyers from smaller stores, Zack would schmooze for a few minutes and call one of the two great salespeople he had trained to sell the collection. Together, they were a selling machine.

My favorite part of market weeks in New York were the late afternoons and early evenings, when all the buyers were gone, and Lee would pull out a bottle of Dewar's whiskey and ice. Zack drank Diet Coke, making him the designated driver. I loved this ritual with Lee and Zack for four seasons every year. It was obvious that Steven got his coaching of going deeper than the surface level with clients from his parents.

At the end of each day, the entire sales team would recap the day and share the reactions to the collection and discuss how many units were sold of every style and how many units they thought they could sell of each dress in the collection.

The quality-control issue was serious. The company was experiencing a ten percent return rate from stores due to poor quality. Fixing this issue became my crusade and I thoroughly enjoyed turning that aspect of the company around.

My often-repeated message was that we must make sure that every single woman that buys Jonathan Martin products must trust our quality in every respect. The mantra was "trust is everything." I was also adamant about providing our customers a perfect fit. I would regularly request the designers to provide extra fabric in certain areas like the waist and under the arms. The stitching had to be high quality without loose threads hanging. The sewing contractors were primarily immigrants. I had a routine when visiting the sewing factories to walk by each sewing station and thank them for being careful while sewing our shirts, dresses, and skirts. I loved the warm response of appreciation from these very hardworking women.

Rose Morone, my understudy, successfully created a system that tracked every single garment that was in production. She ensured that there was a sign-off process by a Jonathan Martin quality-control inspector before the finished goods were sent to the factory for shipping to the stores countrywide. Every single garment that was shipped out of our factory was inspected for quality for the entire time I was at Jonathan Martin.

Around the time I started with Uri, and one year after leaving Australia, Shira, my first and only love up to that point of my life, wrote to me. She had realized that she made a horrible mistake by staying in Australia and wanted to be with me. I expressed to Shira that I had conflicting emotions about her coming to Los Angeles. On the one hand, I was lonely and needed an intimate relationship. On the other hand, I was not ready to commit to her. I had only experienced a few physical relationships in my adult life before the age of twenty-two.

We finally agreed that Shira would move to LA and live with me in a newly acquired apartment building on Rexford Drive in Beverly Hills for one month while we looked for a suitable apartment for her on the west side of LA. She made the courageous move midyear for the applied psychology course at Northridge University, where she eventually graduated with the dean's honors.

Meanwhile, Uri and I decided to embark on a marketing campaign to expose the brand and the concept of career clothing in general. Women were working all over the country in executive positions and they needed fine apparel to enhance their professional look. I vetted several ad agencies, and Young & Rubicam was the only one that I invited for a second interview at the factory. Uri and I did not waste time to sign them on. At that time, Y&R was a public company specializing in advertising and branding and had a volume in excess of two billion dollars a year. They loved our story and wanted to assist in promoting our brand. The copywriter assigned to Jonathan Martin was Neel Muller, who had recently relocated to LA from South Africa. He suggested from the beginning that we should launch the brand with a unicorn as part of the logo. He explained that for many generations women always had an affinity with the unicorn's mystical symbol. We agreed to add the unicorn to our Jonathan Martin logo.

At the same time, we collaborated with Burson-Marsteller, a global public relations and communications firm headquartered in New York City. They were a billion-dollar-plus company closely tied to Y&R. Trudy Rohla was our account executive there and was another guardian angel, even though she represented at least eight Fortune 500 companies. She made me feel that representing our company was her life mission and purpose. She loved that I cared so much about the career woman and she witnessed for herself the garment-by-garment inspection to ensure our A+ quality control. I was driven to provide a great product for the twenty-five to fifty-year-old working woman.

Trudy's role was to humanize the brand. We received a lot of free press talking about the importance of this growing segment of the career woman in our communities. We were regularly interviewed about our opinions on industry news by the fashion authority, *WWD* (*Women's Wear Daily*). We developed an extensive billboard campaign in major markets in Los Angeles, San Francisco, and New York with the same concept throughout each market, showing a model wearing beautiful dresses and blouses with the best tagline of all time: "Nobody dresses a woman like Jonathan Martin." This was Neel Muller's contribution that made our brand official on a much larger scale. Thank you, Neel Muller. I still consult with Neel to this day on the Luxe Hotels brand.

Uri and I warned both mega agencies that we didn't have a huge budget for an extensive ad and marketing campaign. They had to fine-tune their skills, getting us the most bang for our dollar. The term "guerrilla marketing" was used at the time.

Y&R skillfully and strategically evaluated the cities and dates of the five major annual fashion-market-weeks that took place every year. Primarily, twice a year, New York, Los Angeles, Dallas, and Chicago's fashion weeks. They negotiated aggressively on our behalf to run TV ads with the goal of targeting our dress and blouse buyers. The most expensive TV commercials were the CBS Sunday evening news hour at 6:00 p.m. Our ads would run at 6:58 or 6:59 p.m. This was one minute before the highly popular *60 Minutes* program. The cost to run the spot was a tenth of advertising on *60 Minutes*.

Y&R also negotiated aggressively on our behalf to buy spots on the popular morning shows, like *Good Morning America* and *The Today Show*. Many new buyers would walk into our showroom saying that they didn't make an appointment; however, while they were getting dressed that morning, they saw our commercials and wanted to know more and see our collection.

My favorite of the five commercials we created was the attractive male ad. Y&R pinpointed five soft-spoken, handsome men with a variety of cultural backgrounds. It started with each man being closely cropped and looking deep into the camera. First an Italian, then French, German, Swahili, and then an American saying the same thing in each of their respective languages: "No one dresses a woman like Jonathan Martin." The ad was very effective, and people loved it.

For the New York market we added, after the American model, a seventy-year-old bald tailor wearing half-rimmed glasses speaking in Yiddish saying the same thing with a lot of hand motions: "No one dresses a woman like Jonathan Martin." We believed that after seeing the ad showing on TV, on billboards, and in industry press, buyers had an obligation and duty to find out what the Jonathan Martin collection was all about.

Burson-Marsteller orchestrated several New York runway launches of the Jonathan Martin collections. Most memorable was my first one at the Waldorf Astoria hotel in 1983. Fantastic staging, designs with giant reproductions of office supplies like six-foot pencils, three-foot erasers, and ten beautiful models walking between the props. I still remember the speech I gave that day, which was written by Trudy. I had repeated on several occasions that I was a bad public speaker and that I was afraid I might freeze with all the lights, TV cameras, and other individual fashion cameras and major fashion buyers in the audience. I tried to avoid it, yet she insisted I speak. I had to figure out a way to deal with this fear somehow.

This is what I said: "On my way from LA to New York, I happened to sit next to a doctor who was en route to the Bahamas to attend a medical conference. Along the way, we spoke about several subjects. He was saying that the mind is unbelievably powerful and capable of hundreds of thousands of thoughts, whether we are asleep or awake. But it dies on one of two occasions: upon death and when faced with a microphone. I thought this was true, as well. Facing you with the microphone, we welcome you to our launch of our new and exciting Jonathan Martin Missy Division." Once I heard their laughter and applause, I started to get the confidence I needed to speak in public more.

We were building credibility in our product. For me, from the start of my career to this day, credibility is everything. If I lost credibility in any way along the path of getting a finished dress or blouse onto the physical body of my consumer, I believed the business could not be sustainable and would fail in the long term. It was a natural instinct that drove me to choose this path in my business life from the day I started working. Trust is everything.

Despite Zack and Lee's great relationship with the buyers on the East Coast, I traveled to New York regularly. I always wanted to personally deliver our new seasons' dress collections. In addition, I wanted to be present when new lines were presented to our clients to see their reactions with my own eyes, and to also acknowledge gratitude for their faith in our product, year after year.

One aspect of my New York sales trips I did not enjoy was my hotel experience. I tried a multitude of properties including the Waldorf Astoria, the Essex House, the Plaza, the Carlyle, and others. I always felt as though I was just a number. No matter how highly rated the hotels were, they all seemed lacking in genuineness. They were missing that very important ingredient of true individual care. It seemed the only thing the hotel employees really cared about was the size of their tip.

In 1983, my dislike of New York hotels motivated me to buy a condo on 36th Street and 1st Avenue, which I still own. It's on the twenty-first floor with beautiful panoramic views of the East River. When I flew first class to New York, most airlines provided complimentary helicopter service from JFK airport to Manhattan. The helipad was conveniently located on 34th Street and First Avenue, two blocks away from my home. This proved to be another high point in my life. At moments like this, for some unknown reason, my mind takes my attention to my feet and I imagine the torn socks rubbing against the grain of sand or pebbles or whatever it was I stood on when I was a little boy. They connected me with the moment and made me appreciate the beauty of the Manhattan skyline. I thought how blessed and fortunate I was to be able to enjoy the experience of arriving into Manhattan from JFK in thirteen minutes, and many more luxuries and pleasures that humble me when I get to experience them.

During this time, our cash flow was improving. Some years saw gross operating profits increased year-over-year by 300 to 500 percent. Our net profits were spectacular. Uri and I began purchasing real estate, primarily in the downtown LA district. I also personally invested with my brother, Terry, purchasing several trophy commercial real estate deals in Sydney. One of the best purchases Uri and I made in 1982 was a home for my parents in Vaucluse, Sydney. It had an unobstructed, panoramic view of the Sydney Harbour Bridge and the Opera House. It was spotted by Uri's wife, Sally. My parents and all visitors particularly enjoyed the living room, which had floor-to-ceiling clear glass windows. It looked like a giant screen image of the beautiful and natural Sydney Harbour and all its bays. Seaplanes landing and taking off every hour were clearly visible. Massive passenger and cargo ships were also visible coming in and out of the harbor. My parents were extremely appreciative to have this home.

We were off to a roaring decade despite the tough world economy in the early 1980s. Inflation was out of control and interest rates were in the 20 percent range. A lot of commercial properties were being foreclosed on and under pressure from the lenders. There was a lot of distressed debt in commercial real estate mortgages.

One of our clients was Moshe, a successful wholesaler who was also from Israel. He became our third partner in many of our early deals, primarily in downtown LA. I was thankful I had Moshe and Uri focusing on the real estate. My big focus was ensuring that we were maximizing the huge demand we created in mainstream women's fashion.

Personally, I was still obsessed with my success and I still had so much to accomplish. My growing wealth could have led my focus and attention astray. I was extremely conscious of always making good choices that I could be proud of later. The drug scene in the garment industry was prevalent; however, I stayed 100 percent clean and avoided excessive alcohol use. I did not partake in the "garmento" party scene. My daily sixty-minute running routine became a lifestyle. Being healthy and in good physical shape helped me maintain my focus on what was most important at that time. I've maintained the sixty-minute exercise habit to this day.

It was most difficult exercising self-control when I traveled with my dress designer, Helen. We traveled together to look for trends and styles from New York to London to Paris. We were both single and she was very attractive. But we couldn't act on any impulses. There was no time for distractions from my true goal. I was constantly making split-second decisions with the goal of not letting down my guard.

MOVING TO BEVERLY HILLS

In 1982 to 1983, via my friend Harold, my bid was accepted in an estate sale to buy a home on Foothill Road in Beverly Hills. Built in 1927, it was a one-story home with an unattractive stained wood exterior. It was sold as a teardown, but I loved the openness inside the house and the fantastic three-quarter-acre backyard.

In 1985 the house next door to mine on Foothill, also a teardown, was listed for sale. I bought it with the idea that I would build one beautiful home with a tennis court and a swimming pool on the over one-acre lot in Beverly Hills.

Since my youth I have had a mental image of what being twenty-five years old would look like. My goal was that by this age I would have very good cash flow from my business and enough cash that I would buy myself a very special second car with one condition—that I would not borrow a penny.

An opportunity came up to buy a new eggshell-colored Rolls Royce Corniche convertible, with a taupe leather interior. It was a beautiful car. I bought it and I felt like I achieved my goal. Once I purchased the car, I rarely drove it. I was embarrassed to have my downtown factory staff see it. I was even self-conscious driving this beautiful handcrafted car around town in Beverly Hills. However, I got a lot of pleasure driving long distances to Malibu, San Diego, and Santa Barbara. Within a few months, I realized that the type of car I was driving did not give me a feeling of success and self-worth. Success and self-worth are a lot deeper than that. I needed to reinforce my self-worth because material objects would never be able to validate my success.

During these rapid growth years, I made a point of always being connected to the executive team, as well as every single line employee. I constantly expressed gratitude for their hard work and for bringing success. Positive energy throughout the factory was important to engender. I loved working at times with the shipping department, helping them pack merchandise or simply move inventory around. It made them feel like we were still grounded and that I still cared.

GORKY PARK

Living in LA in the eighties made it difficult to avoid being involved in the movie industry. Somehow Uri and I sandwiched the production of two feature films in between manufacturing women's clothing and buying real estate.

The more successful of the two was *Gorky Park*, which was based on a *New York Times* bestseller by Martin Cruz Smith. A neighbor and friend, Howard Koch, encouraged our involvement. He secured Dennis Potter from England to write the screenplay. He also secured incredible actors for the lead roles, including William Hurt, Lee Marvin, Joanna Pacula (she was nominated for the Golden Globe Award for Best Supporting Actress for the role), and Brian Dennehy. The film was a critically acclaimed psychological thriller about a Moscow police officer who investigates a triple homicide and comes across a political conspiracy in the local government.

Next step in the moviemaking process was to find a film studio to commit to the many millions of dollars it would take to make the movie. After months of many studios rejecting the movie, Orion Pictures agreed to finance it.

The original plan was to film it in St. Petersburg, Russia. While the production scouting teams were pulling permits for the film there, the Russian authorities considered the book anti-Russian propaganda. They did not allow the film to be shot there.

Finland was chosen as a substitute, because its weather and architecture were similar to Russia. It was a thrill being on the set in Finland. I particularly enjoyed meeting William Hurt, who had just completed the film *Altered States*. During a lunchtime break from filming, Howard introduced me to William, who I considered one of my favorite actors. I felt a little tongue-tied while we had coffee and a cookie together. He broke the silence by saying, "Thank you for backing this film. The script is great. This is one of my favorite roles ever and I really love this movie."

These few words had an impact on me. He could've said to Howard, "I don't want to be disturbed when I'm in character." I would've gladly honored his wish. But I am very grateful to have had those few moments with him.

Gorky Park had a successful worldwide release in 1983. William Hurt's next film was the major box-office hit, *The Big Chill*.

We dabbled in one more movie called *Ghost Warrior*. Tim Curnen wrote the screenplay in 1983. Half of the movie was spoken in Japanese and subtitled in English. Unfortunately, the group behind the story was not professional and did not create a quality product. The film was released in theaters in 1984. However, it lasted one week in movie theaters before being taken off the screen.

I often expressed gratitude to my good friend and movie producer, Todd Black, who I met in 1980 and who remains a treasured friend today. Todd kept me out of the movie industry and constantly repeated, "If you are an outsider dabbling in the movie industry, you will not succeed. Guaranteed." I listened to Todd's sage advice and despite constant offers, I quote Todd and repeat, "I will absolutely not get involved in the movie business again."

Due to the growth in our overall sales and our net operation income, our CPA warned us that we would be paying half in federal and state taxes. He advised us to invest in a hotel to take advantage of the rapid depreciation and other tax benefits.

So Harold and I went out looking for a hotel. He learned that the Algerian owner of The Hollywood Roosevelt Hotel needed to quickly sell this asset. While Harold and I were doing a site inspection, there was a shooting in the hotel parking lot. I looked at Harold and said, "Thanks, but no thanks!" The next day, Harold discovered that the same Algerian owner had another seven-acre hotel property on Sunset Boulevard called The Bel Air Sands Hotel. Uri and I were enchanted by the property size and its location in the center of Los Angeles, between the San Fernando Valley, Beverly Hills, and Santa Monica. We purchased that property and jumped into the hospitality business.

In the early eighties, my life was very frenzied. I was a partner of an incredibly successful clothing brand, I bought a hotel and was now in the hospitality business, and I even produced a major motion picture! All of those were taking up 200 percent of my time. I had my Rolls Royce Corniche, a beautiful home in one of the most expensive neighborhoods on earth, and I still wanted more! My incessant drive and my constant energy kept pushing me frenetically forward.

GET OUTSIDE OF THE FISHBOWL

I love to quote the saying by John Culkin, "We don't know who discovered water, but it certainly wasn't fish." The fish didn't create the water. It doesn't know anything else because it is always immersed in water, so it doesn't know its context.

In that same way, David, Ben, Uri, Terry, and I, along with the rest of my siblings, were all subjects in our particular context. We saw and learned how to live life and survive through the same similar upbringing and family culture.

I worked hard to get outside that bowl. Getting outside helped me see the many powerful imprints in which everyone in the family got caught up: Always struggling, stressed, the whole world being "on our parents' back." I realize now that these unconscious impressions that we saw, experienced, and registered while growing up still impacts all of us in different ways.

All the male siblings were so driven and obsessed to succeed as businessmen. After thirteen years, Uri and I had amassed trophy portfolios of ten buildings together. Jonathan Martin grew tenfold in volume. The plan worked, but my life seemed to be heading out of control.

Something significant was happening. I began to lose the most important thing in my life: my soul. It is difficult for family members to work together, especially two strong personalities like Uri and me.

All the millions of dollars I was making at Jonathan Martin and the rents I was being paid from my various real estate holdings every month were not enough to get me out of the bowl, to be objective, and to see where I was headed.

A tale I heard resonated with my own life experience. It was a story of a man who had been told that he would be given all the land he could manage to cover on foot in one day. He then ran and ran so as not to pass up the opportunity to acquire one more yard, one more mile, one more acre. When he could run no longer, he managed to crawl. As he finally collapsed from exhaustion, he stretched out his hands, straining to cover yet another few inches. His dying words were, "This, too, is mine." He did not know when to appreciate what he had. We always want more but we must learn to be able to say, "I have enough." Thus, he never got to enjoy the fruits of his labors.

Around this time, one of my most enjoyable acquisitions was my home on Pacific Coast Highway, in Malibu. It was a two-story, five-bedroom white wooden frame American Colonial house perched on a bluff, with a private walkway down to the Pacific Ocean with access to Zuma Beach. I loved it at first glance.

I enjoyed the peace and quiet of Malibu, especially the walks and my meditations by the beach. However, it was there I noticed that I was still like a fish lost in the water. I was blinded by my subjectivity. Once I became aware of my context, I wanted different things for myself.

I discovered this context by learning to meditate. Meditation by the ocean, with the sound of the waves coming and going and wind rustling through the palm trees, was definitely transformational.

I spent a lot of time with good friends in Malibu, primarily Todd Black. I'm grateful that our friendship today is as strong as when we met over thirty-five years ago. Todd has developed a reputation in the movie industry for being a successful, creative, and straightforward movie producer.

The story has not been told enough in the movie industry about a conversation that was struck up one evening with Todd and a Sony studio security guard, whose name was Antwone Fisher. Let me tell you this amazing story:

Todd was in the office late one night, when one of the security guards knocks on his office door and said goodbye to Todd, advising him that he was going to Cleveland to meet his mom for the first time.

Todd wanted to hear more. Antwone explained that he was born in prison, and his birth father was shot dead by a jealous girlfriend. As a result, he grew up in several foster homes, without having known his parents. Twelve years of Antwone's childhood were spent with a couple whose children were already grown. They beat him physically, and he was emotionally neglected. A neighbor and family friend had sexually abused him for many years, and his foster father did not acknowledge whether he even knew his name. After a fight with his foster mother, he was kicked out of the house and returned to social services.

He attended a specialized high school for disadvantaged boys. While at the school he met a social worker who was a positive influence in Fisher's life. Once he graduated, however, he entered the criminal world of Cleveland. His job was to collect money from prostitutes for a local pimp.

Looking to change his life around, he joined the US Navy, where he spent eleven years in the service. He received counseling from the naval psychologist (the part in the movie played by Denzel Washington). The psychologist motivated Antwone to discover his own origins.

After his honorable discharge from the Navy, he became a federal corrections officer for the Federal Bureau of Prisons for three years. Then he began working as a security guard for Sony Pictures Culver City Studio in Los Angeles. And he was determined to discover his biological family.

Todd wished Antwone a safe trip, and he advised Antwone that his was an amazing life story and that he was prepared to help him write a screenplay upon his return.

Fisher sold his first script, with Todd's help, to Sony Pictures for a million dollars. Derek Luke played Antwone in the movie *Antwone Fisher*. Todd was the film's executive producer and he gave Denzel Washington his first directorship.

I met Antwone and his wife at one of Todd's housewarming parties. Following the movie, Antwone Fisher sold two more scripts, published a book, and also released a small leatherbound book of poetry called *Who Will Cry for the Little Boy?*

As a film producer, Todd is blessed with the gift of empathy. In the same way he had the capacity to hear and relate to Antwone Fisher, he heard the depth of my story when we met. He also had one other quality that was extremely endearing to me. He was the only person I know that would refuse my offer to heavily invest in a new movie production company that he was starting at the time. I wanted Todd to invest on my behalf in his new business, primarily by buying and developing scripts. He absolutely rejected the money. He did not want me to invest a penny in the movie industry and he meant it.

Most importantly, Todd helped me become aware of my context. Once that happened, a lot changed for me. He helped me objectively see my background for what it was. It was then that I realized I was very far from my deepest true self.

MY FIRST MEMORY

In order to reconnect with my soul, I had to think back to my childhood. I became aware that I was into the deepest context of those components and had been there since a young age. My earliest memory of being "mature" was at age five in Petah Tikva, Israel. My mother and I were leaving the house to go to the fruit and vegetable market, which was a thirty-minute walk. We left one-year-old Sophie at the house with my grandmother, who was old, feeble, and very hard of hearing.

The walk up the road was rushed from the moment we started. My mom held my hand as we walked, saying we need to hurry and return before Sophie woke up. I was silent in her silence. I was aware of how much pressure she was feeling. Her face looked stressed; the whole world seemed to be on her shoulders. I made sure I kept up with her, despite her longer and faster strides.

Once we arrived at the large, open, and partially covered market, she went straight to her regular vendors. They were happy to see her and spoke to her in our native Iraqi language, as most stall owners were Iraqi Jews. I loved how she would make a face when hearing prices she didn't like. At the same time her hands were checking out the freshness of the vegetables and fruit. She always seemed to get a reduction in price. When certain vendors would not charge her for certain items, her face lit up with appreciation and she would shower the stall owner with a blessing or two.

I felt jealous of all the smiles, words of praise, and nods of appreciation the vendors were giving her. The walk home felt a lot faster despite the load that she primarily carried. I really wanted to lighten her burden, so I also carried some of the bags without a complaint about the discomfort and the rushed pace.

Unfortunately, when we arrived back home, Sophie was standing in her crib, crying at the top of her lungs, to the point that her lips turned purple in color. No one was able to her to hear her or comfort her. It deeply affected me to see my baby sister in such despair.

I was able to recognize my deep imprint etched into the back of my mind: "Don't ever abandon Mom; help her." Another imprint deeply embedded in me is the concept of "Rush." This relates to my constant need to not waste time and be active, which makes me rush through my thoughts and actions.

Whenever I think of my childhood, I immediately think of this moment. It was a rare moment of pure, innocent love for my mom and feeling sorry for all her pain. Despite my joylessness at that moment—the fast walking and carrying—I connected and felt my own self. I felt my true essence, my *neshama* (soul).

I had the capacity for such deep compassion and genuine care in my heart for another. In Hebrew this is called having *rachmanut* (feeling pity). That is what I wanted to reclaim in myself. This is what my good and loyal friend Todd helped me see, this wonderful quality in myself, which I had been unable to see or tap into on my own.

On a recent morning, I called Todd to ask him if I could use his name in this book. He absolutely agreed and added that he was honored. I took the opportunity to thank Todd again, for reigniting my soul on such a deep level.

Todd said for people to understand and know me, they have to be aware that, despite my brilliant business mind and all my success, I approach everything from the heart, and this is why he loved being associated with me. He said that I had equally impacted his life, and that he regularly thinks of me.

Todd closed off by saying I need to realize that I am on the "Top 10" list of people in his life. Those words meant so much to me. We ended with him expressing how much he appreciated my unexpected call, noting it made his day.

A DECISION IS MADE

After fifteen years of working with Uri, with our extremely different styles of behavior, demeanor, and personality, we were no longer behaving like partners. We had stopped discussing each other's ideas and plans for the business. We were arguing constantly and with this breakdown in communication, I needed to figure out how to move on from this partnership.

I felt the straws beginning to stack up on my back. I was no longer able to continue accepting the status quo, now that I had become aware of my context. Before making any final decisions about leaving the partnership, I scheduled a meeting with Sanford Bernstein, the founder of AllianceBernstein, whose company was my personal wealth fund manager and, more importantly, who I considered to be my mentor.

At that stage in his life, Mr. Bernstein was semi-retired and living with his lovely wife, Mem, in the beautiful artist colony, Yemin Moshe in Jerusalem (I currently have a home twenty feet away from the Bernstein residence). To ensure I was not making a huge mistake by walking away from the Jonathan Martin brand, which was still a cash-making machine, I flew to Jerusalem for the sole reason of talking to Mr. Bernstein.

My friendship with Mr. Bernstein was triggered ten years earlier by a meeting we had. Due to his custom of meeting at least one client in LA when he was en route to his Palm Springs residence, I got the call from his assistant in New York to set up a dinner date. I received at least three other calls from his office to remind me that he only ate kosher.

We arranged to meet and have dinner at my then recently acquired Bel Air Sands Hotel. He was in great shape and perfectly dressed in a suit and tie. I was surprised to see that he wore a yarmulke on his head. This was a "wow" moment for me, to see someone as successful as Mr. Bernstein adhering to this strict religious tradition. As we sat and spoke, he primarily spoke about my background and my family story, all while we were eating the delicious lemon sole and grilled vegetables. Toward the end of our meal, he asked me from where I had ordered the delicious kosher food.

I explained to him that his assistant was very concerned that our meal was 100 percent kosher, so I asked my community rabbi, Rabbi Moshe Benzaquen, to supervise that the executive chef used only kosher ingredients and that we dined with all new utensils. Bernstein was surprised and humbled that a community rabbi was supervising our two meals in the hotel kitchen. He asked me to invite him to join us. He was fascinated by the rabbi's roots in Mela, Spain, and by his ability to quote parts of the Torah in perfect, biblical Hebrew. Mr. Bernstein asked Rabbi Benzaquen a barrage of questions. At the end of the evening he inquired, "So what exciting projects are you working on now, Rabbi?" The rabbi explained that he had initiated a Monday Night program six months earlier at his synagogue. The program brings in speakers to discuss a variety of interesting topics for young Jewish singles between the ages of eighteen and thirty. What seemed to get Mr. Bernstein's attention was that this Monday Night program had already resulted in four marriages in the community.

Several days later, Rabbi Benzaquen got a call from New York to arrange a time to meet two individuals working for Mr. Bernstein and asking for more details regarding the Monday Night program. Within approximately two weeks, Mr. Bernstein sent a check for $75,000 to assist the rabbi in continuing this program. Mr. Bernstein's heart was definitely in the right place.

After listening patiently to my update, Mr. Bernstein, without a single ounce of hesitation, advised me that it sounded like it was not a healthy working environment and that I should exit Jonathan Martin. He said when trust is lost in a relationship, especially so in a partnership—it's over. He emphasized repeatedly that he had absolute faith that I should exit the partnership, even if I had to pay for my freedom. There was absolutely no question in his mind.

A few days later I returned to LA from Israel, still weighing the valuable advice to separate from Uri which I received from Mr. Bernstein. Within a couple of days of my return to work with my new context reaffirmed, I began to clearly see how unhealthy it would be for me to stay. I walked into Uri's office and advised him that I could not work in that environment anymore and that I was planning to make that my last day.

He responded, "What are you talking about? *I* am the one leaving the company. I am leaving and I am going to be retiring."

I said, "It's your choice but I'm going to be gone at noon today." I stuck to my boundary and left at midday that day.

As Mr. Bernstein suggested, I actually paid Uri to gain my freedom. To make the separation uncomplicated and speedy, I told Uri that in return for my half share in Jonathan Martin, I would accept his half share of the Bel Air Sands Hotel, which was operating at $100,000 negative cash flow per month. He thought this was not a good deal for him, so he requested that I also deed over to him my half share in two large pieces of commercial downtown real estate. I agreed.

Uri assumed my share in Jonathan Martin and continued to operate it for approximately ten years after I departed.

The separation was not easy. It sent shockwaves throughout our family and we are all working, to this day, to reestablish that lost love. With all that behind us, I look forward to the next chapter in Uri's and my relationship.

During the previous fourteen years in LA, the three years before that at Lulu in Sydney, and throughout my school years, I had lost myself in my roller-coaster race to come out rich. Obviously, making lots of money, struggle, survival, and being mature were important components of what I saw as a child and learned unconsciously.

PILLAR TWO
THE ART OF HOSPITALITY

"Excellence is not an act, but a habit."

—Aristotle

Chapter 4
SUNSET BOULEVARD

FROM THREADS TO BEDS

It was 1983 when Uri and I purchased The Bel Air Sands Hotel—which ultimately became the Luxe Sunset Boulevard Hotel—as an investment. Initially, we thought we would turn the seven-acre hotel property into exclusive condominiums.

Uri had a friend named Tulie, who owned the five-hundred-room LAX Hilton and several other apartment and condo complexes in LA. Uri thought having Tulie's experience could be useful for our hotel. We agreed to invite him to be the third partner on this deal. It all went smoothly until it came time to close escrow. Tulie didn't have the money he had claimed to have had.

I went to the bank that day with my down payment cashier's check for a million dollars, and Uri went to the bank with his portion of the down payment. We waited for Tulie. Tulie didn't show up! Instead, his kids came running into the Manufacturer's Bank in downtown LA—his four boys, aged seventeen through twenty-two—and said, "Dad didn't have the money today, and he wonders if you will cover him for his portion?"

So, here we are, up against the wall. We spoke to the bank manager, Mr. Sam Simons, and asked, "Can you give us an additional line of credit for another million dollars?" He disappeared for ten minutes and returned with a smile that the answer was "Yes!"

A year later in 1985, we asked, "Tulie, where is the money?" His response was, "I want to sell the hotel. I am a third partner. My name is on the title, and I want to sell the hotel." This was in spite of the fact he hadn't repaid us a penny for the million-dollar loan. Unfortunately, we had trusted him, and put his name alongside ours on the title.

He said, "I can sell the hotel right now for double what we paid for it. That would make a great profit, and I can pay you the million, plus interest out of that." But we didn't want to sell at that point, so we ended up paying Tulie an additional million dollars just to get him out of this deal!

Then in 1991, when I left Jonathan Martin, I decided to take the leap into sole ownership of the hotel and made a property settlement with Uri for the "fair value" of my half of Jonathan Martin.

Finally, I was flying solo.

CREDIBILITY IS EVERYTHING

Once I became sole owner of the hotel, I agreed to enter into a contract with a well-known hotel chain, making the Sunset Boulevard property just one more link of that chain. I was hoping they would take over the hotel operations and create a financially successful branded hotel. I was also newly married that year and wanted to give my wife a lot of my attention. But my career only became more demanding, and my retirement from the business was not wholly practical. Within four months the hotel chain had signed up several other hotels in the area, using mine as a sample hotel. They talked the others into converting to their brand by showing them the Sunset Boulevard property as an example.

Unfortunately, they offered no quality control, which negatively affected our rates. You didn't have to be a rocket scientist to see the correlation between our dropping rates and the additional hotels the brand was converting.

I knew I wanted out of my contract. After five years, I mustered the courage to walk out of the contract which was originally signed for fifteen years. According to the terms, the brand could sue me for millions of dollars over the revenues they lost by losing me as a franchisee.

The president of the chain flew in from the East Coast and came to the hotel. We sat in a suite while he told me I was going to bankrupt my hotel by leaving them. I may have seemed calm but inside I was very nervous! But I knew I had to move forward.

I showed him the photograph that I had taken of the missing letter "A" in their sign on the rooftop of another one of their hotels three miles away, further illustrating the lack of care they had for their brand's reputation. It was undeniable evidence that even the president couldn't condone, and that got us out of our fifteen-year contract, only five years into it! I am lucky I used a consulting firm called Warnick + Company and Wayne Williams to help me. I have been working with them for more than twenty-five years now. They have helped me develop and master my brand, as well as my concept of excellence. In addition, they helped me reposition my business in the marketplace. At the moment, I am currently expanding the Luxe Hotels brand with the valuable guidance they provided.

Within thirty days of severing our relationship with the hotel chain, occupancy dropped by about 10 percent, which we anticipated, but within sixty days our rates stabilized. Within twelve months, our rates almost doubled. That recovery was all about focus, getting the sales team aligned, and selling packages. Things were looking promising.

After this five-year experience with the brand, I realized there was a void in the hospitality industry I wanted to fill for the purpose of providing the support and those deeper roots for other independently owned hotels. When the winds are the strongest, we need to have the deepest roots to get us through the most difficult times. I felt unsettlingly strong winds approaching and I was certain there were other owners like me, that needed those deep roots to anchor and help them navigate through the most difficult times in our industry.

I saw clearly the need for a hospitality company that fulfills their promises, one that stands for integrity, quality, and exceptional service. That planted the idea for what would later become the Luxe Hotels.

LOVE THY NEIGHBOR

Shortly after I signed with the mainstream brand, some of the neighbors were up in arms about having a major hotel brand in their quiet, mostly residential neighborhood. I received a notice from Mayor Tom Bradley because of several neighbors' complaints about the hotel. We received an order to "cease and desist" from operating the hotel, restaurant, and bar for non-hotel guests. The notice indicated that the hotel caused an overflow of parking into the neighborhood and that the noise levels were excessive.

It was Councilman Hal Bernson who stood up for me at the City Council when, after several hearings, he said, "What the hell? This guy is just trying to help his business survive. He is showing you his financial numbers and he's telling you he needs that help."

Councilman Bernson was so courageous to have spoken out in my favor because, at the same time, our local councilman was playing politics to downgrade our use of the property as a hotel and making it an apartment-hotel. For me to utilize the seven acres of prime real estate as an apartment-hotel was not going to work—especially with the price I paid for the property. I wouldn't be able to fulfill its potential with this additional restraint, including not being able to advertise it as a hotel. It was to be restricted only to those who stayed at the hotel as guests.

To come up with a solution, I went to meet the neighbors to foster supportive friendships. I literally went around the neighborhood and rang doorbells and introduced myself and inquired into what everyone's problems and concerns were. I was surprised to find out that none of them had any problems with me per se, except for a few retired lawyers and architects, who were miles away from my hotel, but were still vocal. They wanted to slow down my business. They were supposedly "protecting the neighborhood."

I found myself in a position where I had to stand up and fight for my rights, and the zoning of the property. This was my first experience learning how important it is to "love thy neighbor" and create sincere relationships with them. I was familiar with the concept, as I mentioned earlier, from observing my parents develop friendships with various neighbors over the years and knowing how important these relationships were.

I began a campaign with my team to communicate, at all levels of the community, my theory that *a hotel is a living and breathing part of its community.* The concept has been proven repeatedly. When an earthquake hit, gas leaks happened, or fires encroached on nearby neighborhoods, we welcomed the community into our hotels. We ingratiated ourselves to the community by sponsoring simple outreach programs like activities for local schools, such as teaching cookie baking for third and fourth graders.

I do this with my neighbors where I live, as well. This experience has created lifelong friendships with my neighbors. Even though, over the years, some of the neighbors have passed away, I make a point of maintaining my friendship with their families and staying in touch.

The Luxe Sunset Boulevard Hotel has become quite popular in the neighborhood and has developed a very close relationship with the

Brentwood community, including the Brentwood Homeowners Association and other homeowner groups in the area. My team and I are driven to do whatever we can to care for our community. We look for opportunities to welcome our neighbors to the hotel. We regularly sponsor local public schools in various ways. For example, a few years ago, we kicked off a fundraiser to build a playground and plant grass, in place of the industrial tar.

Our hotel team also invites local third- through eighth-graders for different fun events at the hotel several times a year. We arrange for the students to have a behind-the-scenes tour of different departments. Almost always, they particularly like the cookie baking experience with our executive chef. Our goal is to make the children knowledgeable about the function of hotels and not be intimidated by the formalities.

We are a partner of the United Cerebral Palsy of Los Angeles's Respitality Program, which offers parents of children with cerebral palsy a weekend away at a Luxe Hotel as gift. They are true superheroes taking care of their children with special needs so we, in turn, take care of them when they can get away for a weekend. It gives the parents a chance to recharge and take care of themselves so they can be rejuvenated when they return home to their families. The Respitality Program has been able to provide over 2,100 weekend getaways for these deserving parents. The president and CEO, Ron Cohen, and I pioneered this program and we will continue to partner with them for years to come.

I'm also no stranger to ringing doorbells in the neighborhood and dropping off a box of chocolates. I have done that every year just to keep the relationships there. It is a bit of a challenge "cold-calling" people, ringing doorbells, hearing the dogs start to bark in the house and then, when the door is opened, standing there and introducing myself. There I am, with a box of handmade chocolates my chef prepared, and a voice from inside yelling, "Who is it?"

"I am Efrem Harkham, the owner of the Luxe Sunset Boulevard Hotel. I just wanted to introduce myself and say 'hello,' and 'thank you' for being such a great neighbor."

No matter how many times you do it, it's always a little scary at first, and to be honest, I'm still more than a little shy. But there's no substitute for being there. It's an amazingly valuable experience, and ultimately enjoyable. It creates an unbreakable bond, new friendships, and leaves a good lasting impression.

DON'T VOTE ON AN EMPTY STOMACH

For the last fifteen years, our ballrooms at the Luxe Sunset Boulevard Hotel have served as a voting place for the 90049 zip code of the affluent Brentwood community. At this event each year, we get the chance to meet all our neighbors. I see it as an opportunity to spoil them on the way to the voting booth. Our goal was to turn voting in Brentwood into a fun experience. First, we provide complimentary valet parking. As voters enter the lobby, they're welcomed by my general manager and me, along with other executive staff members, while we let them know that the drinks and the delicious food displayed along the way to the voting booths are for them. As our executive chef, Olivier Russo, told a reporter from CBS News, "People should not vote on an empty stomach."

Every Election Day, Chef Olivier offers a full continental breakfast along with fresh fruit and yogurt parfait. At lunch, he creates an assortment of dips and vegetables, Chinese chicken salad, and other finger foods. In the later part of the day, to wow the stragglers and those voting after work, Chef Olivier presents juicy, white-tipped roasted rack of lamb. By giving these delicacies to the community, we provide them with a true "Luxe" experience to let them know that we are part of the community and that we are here to spoil them—and to remind them never to vote on an empty stomach.

In the 2008 and 2012 elections, our voting location was regarded as one of the best in the US for welcoming people, showcasing the voting area, and inviting voters to have a bite or a drink. Over the years, we've even featured entertainment for the voters, including a flamenco guitarist, opera singers, and harpists.

For the 2016 election, we thought a calming influence would be in order, so we had Rachel Jackson, a Beverly Hills yoga instructor, lead an ongoing twenty-minute outdoor yoga session all day long. After the yoga, we arranged for another instructor to lead a five-minute empowerment meditation accompanied by two brilliant sitar players to help calm everyone. I must thank Stefan and Noemi Pollack of Pollack PR and Marketing Group for their brilliant capacity to have our concepts and messages heard, not just locally but also internationally.

In the stressful 2018 midterm elections, I conjured up the idea of having soothing ancient flutes playing in different areas of the hotel, leading voters to the ballrooms where they were voting. We hosted a tea bar from the Art of Tea to serve calming teas that were all handcrafted to truly allow voters to enjoy the voting process at our hotel.

In providing a polling place, my neighbors have a compelling reason to come and visit. This was chronicled in *Time* magazine's November 9, 2012, issue. In the article "Voting with the 1%," Joel Stein reported: "Efrem Harkham, the owner of the hotel, said he was just being neighborly, and that a good neighbor offers his guests a drink. In Bel Air a good neighbor has to step it up a bit." Mr. Stein reported how impressed he was with the overall experience of something as stressful as voting during an election. We provided free valet parking, hors d'oeuvres, Wi-Fi, and election coverage on two flat-screen TVs. We served breakfast, lunch, and light dinner bites for voters who filtered through our ballrooms the entire day that the polls were open. He continued to report: "Voters sat at tables just outside the hotel restaurant, eating their complimentary lunch and talking about the election. Harrison Ford walked by with his 'I Voted' sticker and I was proud to live in a country where people who have played as the president in action movies get special voting privileges." We were very proud of this auspicious coverage for something that we hold very important at the Luxe Hotels: that we enjoy creating a deep sense of community.

J. PAUL GETTY MUSEUM, MY NEW NEIGHBOR

As luck would have it, after I decided to buy my brother's interest in the hotel, I learned that the new Getty Museum was slated to be built right around the corner from the hotel, and it was to be designed by famed architect Richard Meier. This made up for the pain and legal expense my local homeowners' group was giving me. The J. Paul Getty Estate had purchased seven hundred acres of rolling hills in the mountains, less than a mile from our hotel. It is located on top of a hill that is nine hundred feet above sea level with some of the most incredible views of Los Angeles—from downtown to the ocean. After eight years of construction, it opened in 1997 to critical acclaim from the art world.

While the museum was being built, my team would arrange for several hard-hat tours of the construction for business leaders and important members of the community. The museum wanted to begin connecting with its community. On one of my trips during the construction I was introduced to the curator, David Jaffe.

David Jaffe's claim to fame before coming to The Getty was that while at the Museum of New South Wales, Australia, he had gone to an art auction and spotted a painting that was clouded over with dust. The painting was described as an unsigned "Rubens style" painting. He had a hunch that it was a true Rubens, and he was right. He made the winning bid of $300,000, and it is now officially recognized as a Rubens original being worth $40 to $50 million. Jaffe was suddenly catapulted to recognition as an international master art curator. Jaffe became an overnight sensation, and The Getty Museum hired him away from the Museum of New South Wales.

Aware of his fame, I invited David to join me for lunch at the Luxe Sunset Boulevard Hotel. During our lunch, I asked if I could offer him a room at the hotel where he could conduct business while the museum was being completed. He agreed, and the hotel became the place where he considered which art to purchase for the museum. We took each other up on our respective offers. He had priceless artwork delivered to my hotel, and I was fascinated to be present while the boxes were opened and the art was revealed and examined.

It was the most remarkable experience to see those priceless pieces of art from renowned artists including Monet, Degas, and Gauguin handled like they were *shmatas* (Yiddish for "rag-like clothing"). I continue to be grateful for the great relationship with David Jaffe, Peter Tokofsky, Julian Brooks, and The Getty Museum.

The power of art has impacted my world profoundly. Art is inspiring and lifegiving. For me, art is not only pleasing to look at, but at the same time it is so powerful. An artist captures his or her emotions at that very moment. He or she captures time, and documents it. On paper or on canvas the artist is forever there, in that space.

The Getty Museum now attracts a large percentage of our guests. People travel to Los Angeles to view the extraordinary architecture, gardens, and art collections at the Getty. Our hotel is the choice property for artists like David Hockney, Leon Kosoff, and Anselm Kiefer, a German painter. Many of these artists lead this generation's contribution to the art world, concept art, and modernism. Their art is exhibited in all the great museums of the world including, The Museum of Modern Art in NY, The San Francisco Museum of Art, and The

Royal Academy. We are also proud to host many of the out-of-state trustees of The Getty. The Getty has more than eight hundred employees, many of whom regularly come to the hotel's restaurant and lounge. With a location directly down the hill from The Getty, we couldn't be more perfectly situated.

Chapter 5
RODEO DRIVE

THE ODDS OF BUYING A HOTEL ON RODEO DRIVE

People often ask me how I ended up owning the only hotel on world-famous Rodeo Drive. It was nearly twenty-five years ago, and frankly, it happened just by accident.

I'd received an invitation to an exclusive luncheon in honor of Councilman Hal Bernson that was organized by Rick Caruso, who owns The Grove and Americana shopping malls. Hal was the same city councilman who, five years earlier, had championed our zoning battle in the City Council to keep the property on Sunset as a hotel. So, of course, I was one of the people who replied "Yes" to the event being held at an elegant private business club in Westwood.

By chance, the man sitting next to me was a banker, and after looking at my business card, he asked, "So you are in the hotel business?" I answered yes, to which he said, "My bank has a hotel on Rodeo Drive, in Beverly Hills, and we just can't seem to get rid of this note."

"You're kidding," I said with astonishment. I was intrigued. When the lunch ended, I asked him, "Will you have time to go look at it with me?" He agreed and the rest is history.

So sometimes, the act of simply "showing up" can turn your life around. Had I not gone to that luncheon, I might have never had the opportunity to purchase the only hotel on Rodeo Drive. In fact, I usually don't go to these types of events because of my personal shyness. Often, I am stiff-necked and afraid that I will seem foolish and awkward at these events, especially where I don't know anyone. This is one of the many issues I have worked through after all these years. So, when I received the invitation to this luncheon, I simply made the decision to "show up."

When the banker and I went to look at the hotel, I immediately saw the potential in the location, so I did everything I could to find the financial means and subsequently purchased it.

MARKETING RODEO DRIVE

The city of Beverly Hills has only been around for just over 100 years, and yet it has certainly made a lot of noise in that time. The original Rodeo Drive in the 1920s was just a horse bridle path from Wilshire to Sunset Boulevard.

The Rodeo Drive Committee, RDC for short, was created by visionary luxury retail pioneers: Fred Hayman, Dar Mahboubi, Bruce Meyer, and Don Tronstein. These monthly meetings usually gather at the Luxe Hotel Rodeo Drive rooftop meeting room for the purpose of maintaining an ongoing worldwide campaign to market Rodeo Drive as the world's foremost fashion street for tourists and the rich and famous.

The committee is made up of owners of retail spaces and over thirty store managers of the world's greatest brands. I am always impressed at roll-call to be among the managers of Salvatore Ferragamo, Cartier,

Valentino, Fendi, Patek Phillipe, Rolex, Gucci, Giorgio Armani, Louis Vuitton, Bulgari, and Hermes, to name a few.

At my first RDC meeting in 1995, I met Fred Hayman, who was known as the "Godfather of Rodeo Drive." He was an elegantly dressed man, always accented with yellow, the signature color of his Giorgio boutique. He was soft-spoken, charming, self-assured, and always with a beautiful German shepherd at his side.

Over the years I had the pleasure of socializing and getting to know Fred and his life story. He related to me because of his experience in the hotel industry. He arrived in the US from Switzerland at age sixteen and began his career as a waiter at the Waldorf Astoria in New York.

Fred impressed Waldorf Astoria's owner, Conrad Hilton. In 1955, Mr. Hilton invited Fred to relocate to LA to become maître d' at his new upscale restaurant, L'Escoffier, inside the newly built Beverly Hilton Hotel. He immediately became a major success and was promoted to director of catering, and soon after became head of Food and Beverage. He would proudly tell me that the F&B department at the Beverly Hilton contributed 50 percent of the hotel's total revenue, 20 percent higher than average.

In 1961, he and two partners bought a simple fabric and fashion store, Giorgio, on the corner of Rodeo Drive and Dayton Way. This boutique was actually the first luxury store in Beverly Hills.

Using the knowledge he acquired in the hotel business, he pampered his clients in the store, providing a fully stocked bar serving wine and champagne, an espresso machine, couches for lounging, and a pool table. For a touch of a full glamourous experience, he would chauffer clients to his store with a vintage Rolls Royce.

His Giorgio's store became a tourist attraction for many decades. He had a keen talent to nurture relationships, trends, and fragrances. He founded the heavy scented and recognizable perfume Giorgio, which he sold to Avon for $160 million approximately ten years later. Then he started another perfume called 273 Rodeo. This is why we referred to him as a serial entrepreneur. At the RDC meetings, like a learned guru, he patiently emphasized that we need to remember that people come to Rodeo Drive for the experience. They want to be entertained and be part of a scene. He would repeat that we, as a committee, needed to bring to the table newsworthy ideas that would generate international interest.

In one of our committee's brainstorming sessions, Fred conceptualized and created the idea of the annual Rodeo Drive Walk of Style Award. It would be similar to the Hollywood Walk of Fame, but for talented fashion designers. The committee commissioned the renowned artist Robert Graham (Angelica Huston's husband) to create a stainless-steel torso sculpture. Fred personally offered to split the $400,000 cost for the sculpture with the city of Beverly Hills, in order to expedite the process.

The torso is presently located in the center median of Rodeo Drive and Dayton, across from the Louis Vuitton store. There's a bronze plaque embedded onto the sidewalk that features a personal quote and signature of each designer honoree, up and down Rodeo Drive.

In 2003, Giorgio Armani was the first to receive the coveted miniature Rodeo Drive Walk of Style statuette by Robert Graham of the torso sculpture. The 300 block of Rodeo Drive was closed to traffic for the award ceremony and a huge tent was erected. Armani insisted on flying in fifty gorgeous models from Milan to walk down the runway modeling his upcoming collection. Music was performed by Atlanta rappers Outkast. The masters of ceremonies included Sophia Loren, Steve Martin, Michelle Pfeiffer, and Jodie Foster. Armani's personal quote embedded in the bronze plaque read "Fashion and Cinema for Life."

Subsequent award winners include Tom Ford, photographers Mario Testino and Herb Ritts, Donatella and Gianni (posthumously) Versace,

Princess Grace Kelly, Fred Hayman himself, Bulgari, Christopher Bailey for Burberry, and legendary Australian costume and production designer Catherine Martin.

Some of the notable quotes of the award winners featured on the plaques included Princess Grace's quote, "I believe it is right to honor all those who create beautiful things and give satisfaction to those who see me wearing them." The Burberry plaque features the signature of the company's original founder, Thomas Burberry, as well as the brand's core values: "Protect. Explore. Inspire."

In the same year, the committee honored Catherine Martin. Martin's quote, which is one of my favorites, said: "Fashion has allowed me to follow my dream down fashion's yellow brick road all the way to Rodeo Drive."

The Walk of Style has become a tourist destination and the quotes are seen by a million visitors that come to Rodeo Drive each month. It's a wonderful way to illustrate the creativity and talent that makes Rodeo Drive an international fashion icon.

DANCING IN THE STREET

In 2014, we had a wonderful one hundredth anniversary celebration on Rodeo Drive commemorating when Beverly Hills broke away from Los Angeles and was officially incorporated as a city. The city planned celebratory events throughout the year to celebrate to keep that anniversary top of mind.

I proposed to the City Council of Beverly Hills that we—the Luxe Rodeo Drive Hotel staff—would have a role in this gala celebration. Part of my team's plan was to bake a spectacular, gigantic, record-breaking cake for the entire community to share. So, as part of the festivities, we baked a cake for fifteen thousand people. The incredible sculpture of the cake was designed to look like the original 1932 Beverly Hills City Hall and was absolutely amazing to behold. It was a kosher chocolate cake, no less, so the Jewish residents of Beverly Hills could enjoy it as well.

I was introduced to Chef Donald Wressel of Guittard Chocolate, by the famous pastry chef, Sally Mueller, to supply the chocolate for the sculpted cake. To make the 15,000-slice cake, it took 262 pounds of flour, 460 pounds of sugar, and 900 eggs. The finished cake weighed four tons.

In the weeks leading up to the celebration, the city had been looking for a talent to perform at our Beverly Hills celebration. While several names were in the works, the Rodeo Drive Committee decided on Martha Reeves (of Martha & The Vandellas fame). Martha sang her 1960s Motown hit "Dancing in the Street," while Beverly Hills mayor Lili Bosse and thousands of people literally danced to the music on Rodeo Drive. The event culminated in a five-hour celebration in which Rodeo Drive was blocked off from traffic. It was quite impressive to see fifty thousand people gathered in one place to celebrate. But we did it.

The cake-cutting event became a viral sensation and got over 800 million media hits. Additionally exciting was that the image with me, Martha Reeves, the Lili Bosse, and the giant cake was shown on the New York's Times Square electronic billboard. It was nothing short of spectacular. I was identified on the billboard as the owner of the Luxe Rodeo Drive Hotel, which was great exposure for my flagship hotel location.

Most of all, it made me very proud. That was a perfect example of using creative, authentic marketing to promote the Luxe Hotel brand, Rodeo Drive, and the city of Beverly Hills.

Marketing my Luxe Rodeo Drive Hotel correctly is a key to its success and requires a well-executed concept—one that takes the neighboring brands into account. The street's elegant and beautiful holiday décor, the Baccarat chandeliers lighting the center divider, and everyone dressed up to go shopping makes me feel that we are on one of the most elegant streets in the entire world. Ten million visitors to Rodeo Drive every year would agree.

In my building on the 300 block of Rodeo, there are three very elite tenants: Michael Kors, Rolex, and Patek Phillipe. Having these stores rent space in my building is further reinforcement that it is a high-end property, and our marketing must reflect that image.

Just as I did in Brentwood, when I first began my marketing efforts, I visited all the neighboring stores on Rodeo Drive: from Cartier, Valentino, Giorgio Armani, to Gucci and Fendi. I fostered a personal relationship with each store, and I visit the stores and their management regularly. I found that developing relationships with the people who are the neighbors of your business creates the same kind of lasting bond as in any neighborhood. It makes us feel like we are all striving toward the same goal. We are all located on the same famous street, so we may as well know each other and celebrate the synergistic qualities we share with our world-famous brands.

Chapter 6
A DREAM AND A VISION

INSPIRED BY THE MAGIC OF DISNEY

Just like Walt Disney brought magic to the film business, it is my desire to bring magic to the hotel world. *The Los Angeles Times* published an article, "Putting Magic in Hotels," in July 2011. It featured my story, my hospitality philosophy, and the announcement of the grand opening of The Luxe City Center Hotel. I mentioned in that article that Walt Disney was one of my heroes.

I am amazed how Walt Disney developed his animation company into a global empire. When Walt began in the early 1920s, there were over fifty animation companies. What set him apart was how he sprinkled magic into the cartoons he created. I needed to sprinkle my own magic on my various businesses. In the 1950s Disney made it his mission to create the "Happiest Place on Earth," and he called it Disneyland. Having a dream, creating a goal, aligning the capital, and making it happen is an inspiration and a motivation. Disney's story motivates me to think creatively. His story also illustrates that if you have the right vision and drive, there will always be room for one more player in the business. If you have the magic, it will allow you to shine and stand apart from the others. But the magic must come from real beliefs and true values. That's what makes it magic.

LUXE IS A FEELING

The atmosphere at Luxe Hotels must effuse joy and good energy. The lighting dim or bright as required. Appropriate beautiful music played throughout the day—setting the mood. Our guests must be made to feel very special. The Luxe good feeling can come from a personalized airport pickup, a drink offer at check-in, a housekeeper who finds a lost bracelet, or simply a smile at the front desk. Many of our competitors charge more, offer less, and often discount the importance of taking care of each guest as an individual with their own specific needs and personality.

We came up with a winning formula that includes elevating and empowering all our employees, because hospitality begins and ends with the employees. We strive to create a happy, healthy team environment through training and careful hiring practices and provide them with all the tools they need to service every guest. Our employees are valued, happy hospitality providers and they are proud of what they accomplish every day, with every guest. As one of our team members recently explained, "Luxe is a feeling" that they not only feel, but also impart to the guest as well.

Dale Carnegie's quote, "A person's name is to that person, the sweetest, most important sound in any language" holds true in every business, especially hospitality. Guests love to hear their name mentioned as they arrive at the hotel because it makes them feel like individuals. They, in turn, remember the names of our employees who have seen to their comforts and actually ask for those employees by name upon their return. We anticipate what will make their stay better. Whether it's offering them lozenges if they are coughing and sound like they have a cold, or surprising their child with a plate of cookies and milk, we're on top of it. We look for opportunities to interact with the guests.

I like to make my staff feel that they are being educated in how to do their jobs better. It must be a seamless experience, embedded in the fabric of what we are offering in every aspect of our services and with every interaction we have.

Happy employees. Happy guests. Higher ADRs (Average Daily Rates) and occupancy. It's all connected. And all three are required for a completely successful hospitality experience. My team and I have a mission to share with other hoteliers the lessons we have learned. Some know these lessons already, but it's about not forgetting, maintaining constant consistency, and always expecting excellence from every single team member.

At Luxe Hotels, we go above and beyond to listen to our guests. We remember that every person who enters our hotel brings something new and different, a unique journey and experience, a world of their own. Our job is to recognize and to respect that journey and that world in every interaction. That is the essence of our brand. Luxe to us means "light" and we bring light to our employees, guests, and our community.

NO MAN IS AN ISLAND

Relationships are a crucial part of the business world. They drive careers, sales, and company growth. Just as in life, in business it's imperative to connect with others, and it's impossible to go it alone. Often, one association can lead to many others. I have found that my relationships with peers and colleagues have led to a wealth of friendships, as well as a very valuable and treasured list of contacts who have ultimately benefited everyone in that network. No man is an island. I have worked very hard to create and nurture relationships in all aspects of my life—from friendships to business partnerships. I have experienced personal and professional growth as a result of people and the relationships with them—especially employees, vendors, and satisfied clients. In the hotel business, many companies offer products and services that their competitors also offer; so, a business needs something that will make it stand out. Yet the experience that is provided for the client is the foundation of the relationship and the basis for its loyalty.

Relationships are like muscles—you have to work to develop them and should always use them with authenticity and genuine goodwill. This last quality—goodwill—is of infinite benefit in any situation, but it can only be generated and acquired when a relationship is engaged in an honest way. With that, goodwill can lead to so many positive situations and associations.

I have met and worked with many people during my career, at some of the most influential companies in the world. If I don't personally know someone at a company, then chances are someone in my network does. We are all part of the same team, and these relationships we have developed have benefited everyone involved. It is very gratifying and a great privilege to be part of this exclusive network. It really makes a difference for our hotels.

Many of my relationships have begun by simply showing up, paying attention, and connecting personally with family, business associates, clients, neighbors, and the community members. Relationships are everything. It's important to build that network and to keep expanding it. To clearly explain how important relationships are to me, I refer to my relationship with Barbara Shore as great an example of the importance of "showing up."

I met Barbara Shore in the mid-1980s. The American Society of Travel Agents was holding an event at my hotel, and Barbara was there as their executive director. The Society had thousands of travel agent

LIVING THE LUXE LIFE

My parents, Nagi and Aziza. Baghdad, 1940.

Family picnic in Centennial Park. Sydney, Australia, 1969. (L–R) My siblings, Rebecca, David, Terry, Sophie, my father Nagi, and my mother Aziza.

Efrem with pattern maker Lola Jewsuwun.   **Uri with design assistant Christy Gifford.**

Uri, left, and Efrem Harkham outside their Los Angeles clothing factory.

The brothers in front of their Bel Air Sands Hotel.

In his teens, Efrem was not attracted to sports. He tried them briefly, but turned his back on them. "That wasn't enough for me," he explained. "It wasn't my style — our style. We were all serious, career-oriented people who were expected to make something of ourselves." His eldest brother, David, who had more than 30 stores in Sydney and Canberra, was a driving force.

"I was very proud of him," Efrem said. Still studying law at Sydney University, Efrem began skipping lectures to moonlight in the fashion business and two years later, at the age of 20, he founded Lulu of Australia which he and Uri later sold to another brother.

"I knew a manufacturer who had over-projected on women's shorts," Efrem recalled. "I took a chance and ended up selling 500 to 600 pairs a day. I realised I could relate to that woman. I understood her and I started manufacturing my own shorts . . ."

Uri put in his share of hours in David's business and despite Efrem's work ethic, he subscribed heavily to the theory that

March 11, 1985

all work and no play made Uri a dull boy.

"I met some beautiful people," he said. Among them was Sally Marie, a New Zealander who became his wife and mother of Jonathan Martin. The three of them ended up in the US during a world trip. They had run out of money and Uri, too proud to ask the family for help, went to a Los Angeles garment manufacturer begging for a job in the firm's shipping department.

"He wouldn't give me a job, but he took a liking to me," Uri recalled. "He told me I should stay . . . and gave me some fabric he didn't want. Suddenly I was in business."

Ten years later Uri and Sally Harkham have a Malibu beach-home and a nearly completed Beverly Hills mansion. Now Jonathan Martin is part of a growing Harkham Enterprises empire that includes valuable real estate holdings and the elegant Bel Air Sands Hotel in the fashionable area of Los Angeles.

The brothers also have moved into Hollywood, financing the Lee Marvin Moscow-set thriller *Gorky Park* which Uri admits has more than slaked his thirst for

gambling. "It's a very big gamble but so is the apparel business," he said with relish. "Our batting average is only 50-50, but we are learning and we have the drive and business experience to succeed."

"Both of us are very people-oriented and most of our ventures, like the hotel, are people related," Efrem said.

There are downsides to the Harkhams' American success and perhaps the worst is homesickness for Australia which, like so many who have given up one homeland for another, they embrace passionately.

Both maintain homes in Sydney and have refused repeated offers to sell.

"It's a big problem," Uri said. "I get down there and I don't want to come back. It gets in the way of expanding my real estate holdings here . . .

"It gets so bad I will fly down for the weekend. I get a direct flight Wednesday night which gets me in Friday, and I get the Sunday night flight back."

And the reaction of their father to their American success? "Oh," Efrem said proudly, "he thinks we've made a promising start."

WOMAN'S DAY 29

Headline feature article in *Woman's Day*, March 11, 1985. Article by Peter McDonald.

My childhood friend, Fred Small, with my three-year-old son Aron and me. Beverly Hills, 1997.

Todd Black, a lifelong friend. Director and producer of films such as *Antwone Fisher, Fences, The Equalizer,* and *The Magnificent Seven,* to name a few. Los Angeles, CA, 1986.

David Singleton (L), Getty Museum Group Sales and Tourism Director (and fellow Aussie), and dear friend Peter Tokofsky (R), Getty Museum Senior Public Programs Director. Los Angeles, CA, 2017.

Rabbi Yigal Kutai, Director of the Heritage Center in Hebron, Israel. Beverly Hills, CA, 2006.

My nephew Richie, Sugar Ray Leonard, and me. Luxe Hotel, Sunset Boulevard, Los Angeles, CA, 2011.

William Hurt and me on the set of *Gorky Park* in Helsinki, Finland, 1983.

Meeting President Ronald Reagan in his office at Fox Plaza in Los Angeles, CA, 1992.

My sons, Aron and Benjamin, as toddlers. Beverly Hills, CA, 1998.

My daughter Natalie, three years old. Beverly Hills, CA, 2010.

Luxe Hotel, 360 North Rodeo Drive. Beverly Hills, CA, 2018.

The Luxe Hotel on Sunset Boulevard, by the terrace area, located in front of the ballrooms. Los Angeles, 2018.

Luxe City Center, the first Luxe licensed hotel, located across from the Staples Center, downtown Los Angeles, 2018.

Lotte New York Palace Hotel, on 51st and Madison Avenue, is Manhattan's iconic luxury hotel. New member to our Luxe Collection. New York, 2019.

The Lenox, a landmark hotel in the heart of Boston, and a member of the Luxe Collection. Boston, 2019.

At the launch party for the Luxe Rose Garden Hotel in Rome. Italy, 2019.

Luxe Rose Garden Hotel in Rome, located near Via Veneto, is the first Luxe branded hotel in Europe. Ribbon-cutting ceremony with its general manager and owner, Alessandro Lucio Massari. Rome, Italy, 2019.

The ribbon cutting for the seventh Hark Angel School, which was built in Myanmar. April 2019.

Richie Harkham with students at a recently built Hark Angel School. Mandalay, Myanmar, June 2018.

Award-winning Harkham Wine. Preservative-free Shiraz at the vineyard in Hunter Valley, Australia. November 2017.

My son Aron and Diana's wedding with my siblings. (L–R) Uri, David, Ben, Terry, Rebecca, Sophie, and Sue. Front row: Myself, Aron, and Diana. New Jersey, 2017.

members, so when I saw their event was on the weekly Hotel Events Calendar, I made a point of attending and introducing myself.

I deliberately introduced myself to Barbara in order to personally thank her for bringing this event to my hotel, even though I had yet to remodel the ballroom at that time, and it was rather ugly and drab then.

Barbara tells the story of our meeting:

Before the incredible renovation years ago, the ballroom left a lot to be desired, but the service was so good, I could not resist! I brought many events there because of Judith Feldman (who still works at Luxe Hotels for the last twenty-five years) and the catering team's unmatched caring and quality of service. When Efrem walked into my event that first time, I thought he was the general manager. I remember thinking to myself, "This guy is a really good general manager, to come over to introduce himself, and to see how we are doing." That almost never happens at any hotel. I took his photo with the officers of the organization for publication in a travel trade magazine. When I called the hotel to get his proper title, I learned he was actually the owner of the hotel! I was truly impressed!

After that encounter, we got together for lunch now and then. I had no family living here in Los Angeles, so being welcomed into Efrem's circle and family was amazing. I love being invited there for Shabbat dinners and the Jewish holidays like Passover and Jewish New Year.

Throughout the almost thirty years I've known Efrem, I've watched him build relationships like this repeatedly. He not only gives those he befriends an opportunity to be the best they can be, he often teaches and nurtures them along the way.

When he connects with someone personally or professionally, there is no end to his genuine desire to help them in any way possible. We rarely find such inspiring people as we navigate life. I feel very fortunate, indeed, to have found this friendship.

Barbara has been a wonderful friend to me for many years. All from the chance meeting years ago where I "showed up." This reinforces my belief in the importance of showing up, and most importantly, developing and nurturing the relationships that "pop up" when I do show up.

Chapter 7

BIRTH OF THE LUXE COLLECTION

CREATING AN INTERNATIONAL MARKETING SOLUTION

After the negative experience with the hotel chain, I was very concerned with our hotels' worldwide representation in sales. Six months after I broke away from the chain, my team and I were wooed by a smaller German hotel chain. This relationship provided the same old story. Many promises, but little return. After three years with the German chain, I attended their annual conference in Singapore to have the opportunity to have meetings and review strategies that would help my business. Instead, they shouted, pep-rally style, about how we were "Winners! Winners! Winners!" I felt a deep disappointment because, essentially, I did not feel like a winner, nor was my voice heard by this chain, and my counterparts and I did not have a forum to express our concerns and discontent with their lack of attention. I did not join this chain for inspiration, I joined it for the bottom line. Instead they left us with nonsensical "Rah, Rah, Rah!"

I decided to stop complaining and fix the problem. I needed to do this on my own.

In fact, even while I was thinking of transitioning from the garment business to the hotel business, I drew upon my knowledge in what I liked about some hotels and what I didn't like about others. I would often go to source fabrics in Japan, a major manufacturer of silk-like commercial fabric. This was all before China and South Korea got into the fabric marketplace.

While in the US and other international cities, I would stay at these fantastic hotels that have so much to offer, and yet they weren't being marketed properly to mega travel consortiums and national and international corporations. Experiencing these hotels in great locations, I was already thinking, *There is a void here! They need help.*

FILLING A VOID

Observing the hotels' discounted rates and lack of consistency, I saw a niche to get into the global hospitality business. Most were so clearly not operating at optimum capacity and needed marketing assistance.

I spotted that weakness as characteristic of independent hotels and sensed that I could ultimately do something to improve the way they conduct business. I saw the void, and when I see a void, I consider it to be an opportunity. We all need an opportunity to make a break.

I eventually found that other hotel brands didn't know the travel professionals as well as we did! There was obviously room in the market for a hotel representation company that honored their promises, so I decided this was an opportunity to create an international collection of independently owned hotels that we could market together worldwide.

At the end of the conference in Singapore, I called my lawyer and asked him to immediately place an ad in *Hotel Business* magazine indicating we were looking worldwide to purchase a boutique hotel representation company.

Hotel representation companies provide global sales and marketing services as well as a robust reservation system. As a result of the ad we placed, I purchased three companies: one in New York City, another in Latin America, and a third in Sydney, Australia. Combined, they represented three hundred hotels. We then launched the Luxe Worldwide Hotels (currently named Luxe Collection), a global hotel representation company.

I contracted all three past owners of these companies to stay on for a minimum of three years to assist me to manage the business. The owner of the company I purchased in Australia, Fiona Rose, is still working with us for almost twenty years.

A PERSONALIZED APPROACH

We determined what each hotel needed. More corporate business? More leisure travel agent business? Each hotel is unique, so we focused the team on that individuality and delivered what each hotel needed. We had a promise log, made up of concrete and measurable goals, and we told them we would meet our promise to them. No more empty promises for our hotel members.

To measure our performance, we have a six-month review survey for our hotel clients, asking how we are doing and how is their account manager doing? We want them to know we intend to meet our obligations and commitments to each property.

We've established offices in key cities; Los Angeles, New York, Shanghai, Sydney, Sao Paulo, London, Paris, Milan, Frankfurt, and Madrid. We have staff stationed in those cities to take care of our hoteliers' needs. They introduce our hotel members to corporate clients in that region, or to large travel consortiums such as Frosch, Travel Store, Altour, Valerie Wilson, First In Service, Travel Leaders, Pro Travel, and Carlson Wagonlit, or American Express Travel—the biggest travel provider in the industry. We offer contacts to over fifty thousand travel professionals worldwide.

Our staff opens doors for small hotels like those I own. When we want to promote the hotel on Rodeo Drive, Sunset Boulevard, or Rome to the Sydney marketplace, we contact our office in Sydney. They set up appointments and create an itinerary to meet with leisure travel agencies and corporate clients to market our hotels.

The Luxe Collection is a resource for each of our independent hotel members. We become their extended team. We are there to promote them all around the world. We align them with the right people and give them a platform to have a spotlight on the world stage. These are the kinds of introductions that independently owned hotels can't develop on their own. This is where we come in. When hotels affiliate themselves with the Luxe Collection, they are part of the family and can take advantage of our network of experts.

Our mission is to get hotel owners internationally to understand the benefits of being able to partner and cross-sell as a group of beautiful and elegant hotels. My team and I often explain to our prospective hotel members the "why" behind the company. It is simply to help other independent hotel owners navigate the muddy waters I had already come through. It is easy to tell the story because it is genuine and comes from the heart.

GLOBAL REPRESENTATION

Hospitality has become so sophisticated, and the competition is so powerful and constantly growing, merging, or developing new brands. A hotel must be on top of its game, round the clock, in order to survive. That is what I do: I help all these individually owned hotels to be on top of their game.

It begins with a hotel becoming a client of our representation company, the Luxe Collection. We provide the best-in-class booking engine, personalized account management capabilities, and marketing support for each hotel individually. Member hotels are also promoted in other markets worldwide. We provide our member properties an undisputed global sales advantage through our international sales offices, and my team and I commit to maximizing business opportunities for each of them. Each member hotel also benefits from an extensive variety of valuable reservations services, all of which increase each hotel's viability, visibility, and sales.

Each property, anywhere in the world, maintains its unique identity and remains steadfast in upholding their independence through our tailored services that meet each property's individual needs.

You may think all the above is just "about the money." Yes, financial gain is important; however, it's also about teaching my deeply felt concept about giving, helping, and doing good deeds. It's about genuine hospitality.

All the hotels that we represent under our Luxe Collection are truly the most beautiful hotels around the world in the best locations, offering the highest levels of service, and I am proud that we have a hand in guiding these hotels to strive for that level of excellence.

Chapter 8
LUXE HOTELS

BUILDING A BRAND

When I had the Jonathan Martin clothing line, I worked with gifted art director Neel Muller of Young & Rubicam, one of the top advertising agencies in the world. When I decided to make hospitality my new career, I asked Neel to come up with a four-letter name for my hotel brand, as many of the most recognizable brands in the world—like Coke, Sony, and Nike—have four letters.

I said to Neel, "It should be a promise of quality. It has to be something we can put in front of an existing hotel name." He came up with a list of possible names, including the name Luxe Hotel, the eventual winner. Luxe is a great name. It's solid and it's got the promise of quality.

A book I recently enjoyed reading is *Shoe Dog* by Phil Knight. In its pages the founder of Nike explains that when he had to decide on a new company name, one of three final choices was "Nike." Before he made the selection, he thought, "All iconic brands—Clorox, Xerox, Kleenex—all have short names with two syllables or less. They always

have a strong sounding letter like a 'K' or 'X' that sticks in the mind."
It looks like both Nike and Luxe made the right choice for their brand
names.

Once I had the Luxe name, growing the hotel brand concept
became an obsession for me. I quickly sprang into action and began
registering it in as many places and territories as we could. My team
and I continue to protect it, as we have a policing mechanism to keep
anyone from using the Luxe name in the hotel world. I never imag-
ined I would spend close to five million dollars to date in protecting
this mark from being copied. Since the creation of Luxe Hotels, it has
become synonymous with exclusivity and quality. Every time a hotel
company attempts to use it without authorization, we fight to keep
the name. According to Luxe COO Joy Berry, "Just like there cannot be two Marriotts or two Hiltons, there cannot be two Luxe
Hotels." In the early years, this happened regularly, where hotel
companies tried to use a derivative of the Luxe hotel name. We would
fight and win every time.

But aside from our name, we have other aspects that make us memorable. Delivering excellence at every level and providing comfortable
accommodations that people will remember, appreciate, and return to
again and again has become our brand's unique formula. And it works!

So many hotels seem to be operating strictly as moneymaking enterprises, without the concept of presenting an oasis where guest comfort
and needs are the prime concern. When a hotel communicates that it
only cares about cutting costs and improving profits, genuine care for
guests goes right out the window.

It is often difficult to convince the owners of independent hotels
that they should join our Luxe Hotels chain. The owners of hotels we
approach are initially completely shocked in the psychological fear of
giving up their identity. Adding our brand identity is naturally
intimidating.

My team and I often help potential clients overcome this psychological hurdle by adding the brand name of "Luxe" to their existing name. This allows them to keep their brand name and have the added association of the "Luxe" brand. The perfect example of this came with what we did for the Luxe Rose Garden Hotel in Rome.

Our mantra is "Combining timeless hospitality with smart service." The result is that Luxe Hotels become like your home away from home, but better, offering a welcoming experience of casual luxury.

An independent hotel can easily get lost in the shuffle. That's when we come in to convince a property owner to reposition their hotel in the marketplace. In 2009, I found an owner of a 200-room hotel in downtown LA, across from The Staples Center. The owner was also looking to upgrade his hotel and join an upscale hotel brand. The Luxe City Center became the first Luxe brand hotel not owned by me. It has been ten years that this hotel has been proudly flying the Luxe flag!

THE TEST OF ANY BRAND'S STRENGTH IS ITS ABILITY TO RECOVER

I learned a valuable lesson when I went to my doctor's office for my ten-year physical examination. One of the exercises was to get on a treadmill. I asked the doctor supervising the test, "Are you attempting to see how strong I am, or is it about my endurance?"

He said, "No. Neither one. It is about your capacity to 'recover' from the workout. It is not about your power or your pace; what we care about is your ability to recover." So, in the same way that my doctor cares about my body's ability to recover, I care about each of my hotels being healthy enough to quickly "recover."

Over 40 percent of hotel sales in 2010 involved hotels that were either foreclosed upon or under financial pressure from their lenders. Being part of the Luxe brand, hotels can decrease their worries that this will happen, as they will constantly have the focus and culture of genuine customer care and loyalty. The Luxe brand helps for a quick recovery. We have been extremely fortunate with how quickly we were able to bounce back whenever a downturn has taken place. Rather than close, or lay off team members, or reduce amenities, we instead added new amenities and more value. Being nimble and able to come up with programs, packages, and ideas is what keeps us and our affiliated hotels moving forward. During recessionary times, we make sure guests receive great value for every dollar they spend with us.

Hotels are like airlines; every day, spaces must be filled in order for it to be profitable. Once the flight begins or the day begins, the opportunity to fill that seat or room is lost forever. The idea behind either business is to attract the return visits of our loyal guests, as well as attract new ones. Should there be an emergency or natural disaster, our goal is to transform the experience into an opportunity to bond with and to nurture an even closer relationship with the clients.

One of the aspects of hospitality in which we at Luxe Hotels excel is communicating to our hotel members that they are part of a well established and supportive entity. Our teams are constantly trained to be creative and caring industry professionals. The individual hotel is no longer a stand-alone operation; instead it becomes part of a team of highly trained hotel experts. We give them the security that there is someone looking out for them, and if they face an emergency, they can count on us for solutions.

I have found from the inception of my business life that one of the hardest parts of having a business is "being found." Whether you are in manufacturing, a retailer, or a hotelier, you need to be on top of mind, remembered and then easily found in the marketplace.

Consequently, my team invests a sizable amount of our annual marketing budgets into search engine optimization. Our hotel websites are constantly upgraded so they are at the top of search engine searches, and powerful enough to quickly and easily take reservations at any of our hotels—with a maximum seven clicks of the mouse.

Despite constantly collaborating and expanding to new ventures, my goal is to maintain my independence, be involved, and never to sell out to giant hotel brands with a cookie-cutter mentality.

THE STONELEIGH AND THE LUXE BRAND

The Stoneleigh Hotel, a historic property in Dallas, Texas, joined the Luxe Hotels brand in 2010. It is a beautiful hotel that has been at the same site since 1920. Before my Luxe team stepped in, The Stoneleigh was heavily dependent on business coming in from OTAs (online travel agents). Business was consistently in the red.

My team was able to convince the owner that we had the expertise required to turn around the hotel's profits and to obtain the revenue that they deserved. They trusted us, and the hotel became the Luxe Stoneleigh Hotel, Dallas.

When we got there, we realized the staff was unsure of the fate of their hotel. Their service showed their lack of confidence in both their jobs and the future of the property. We became Stoneleigh's sales and marketing representatives for six months. This gave us the opportunity to polish it up and prepare the team to step up to the Luxe Hotels' standards. We educated the staff as to what we expected from them under this new brand association. Through a series of training sessions, we brought the concept of the brand's culture to their team, educating and communicating with the staff to meet the Luxe standard of excellence, warmth, and hospitality. My team explained to all the employees at the Dallas property how proud we are of the word "Luxe" and that I want to ensure that each of the hotels with which I am affiliated adheres to this level of caring and service. I always want to make sure that we are represented correctly. We let them know that we wanted the same level of service and enthusiastic integrity from the entire staff.

I insisted on meeting every member of the staff, from the dishwashers to the front desk clerks.

Once we explained our goals and standards to everyone, it literally "turned a light on" in everyone's imagination. After that, the hotel started running like it was on fire with enthusiasm. In fact, when the owner, Randi Torres, came in to the hotel, he said, "I don't even recognize the staff. The same people had been serving me for years, and suddenly they seemed totally different!"

This was because we gave them the one thing that they were missing. We gave them hope. We shared our vision. And we implanted our values.

Suddenly, the staff was so excited to come to work because they had pride in what they were doing. They could see that they were making a difference in other people's lives. The change in them was incredible. Previously, they were just going through the motions of hospitality that was expected from them. That's how values and a true mission create the magic, and keep it going every day.

Unifying the staff and making them feel like they are part of a family is imperative. I try to balance a warm and caring demeanor with a tough-love mentality. In short, I try to make each member of my team feel like a family member.

Furthermore, I am very detail oriented and meticulous, as often the best way to complete a task is through consistency and precision. I remind my team, "It's OK if you have to go back to basics." It's about the essentials and the details. "God is in the details," as the saying goes. During the three years I worked with the Luxe Stoneleigh Hotel, I communicated that passion and that same caring to the team in Dallas.

I will never forget the two days preceding the ribbon-cutting ceremony in Dallas and its inauguration into the Luxe Hotels brand. Despite its thirty-six-million-dollar renovation completed three years earlier, the hotel was morbid, grim, and lackluster. Former Luxe Hotels executive vice president, Barbara Shore, was with me for that adventure.

Barbara recalls, "It was just not happening. There was just no sparkle or spark to what we found there. So, we went out that day, in the 103-degree Dallas heat, looking for candles, frames, flowerpots, artwork to hang, and other things to make it look more appealing and alive for the opening night. We arranged topiaries and a red carpet to liven up the entrance, creating an elegant arrival. Everything we did made a gigantic difference for an exciting and very successful opening night party."

My Los Angeles sales team went into the surrounding Dallas community, visiting all the key travel professionals in the area. We met with community leaders, and I visited the Dallas Jewish Federation and brought a case of Harkham wine to let them know about the hotel.

I was amazed to find that some people in the neighborhood, even those who were located only a few blocks away, were unaware that The Stoneleigh Hotel was still operating. I intended to elevate The Stoneleigh back to prominence.

We arranged tours of the magnificent meeting rooms with their wood carved walls from England that were deconstructed and shipped to Dallas in the early 1920s. We invited over two hundred American Express meeting planners from all over the US to join us for breakfast, along with other prominent Dallas-based travel giants, including Virtuoso Travel, Frosch, and others.

We turned this hotel from a property that was in the red to one that made it desirable for the owner to be in a position to sell it. It was a bittersweet success story. On one hand, it was a compliment that we had done our jobs so well that it made the hotel an extremely desirable property. However, the expertise that we imparted to them ultimately caused us to lose the property when, after three years of excellent financial results, the owner sold it to a fund that was restricted to only permit Marriott, Hilton, or Sheraton as a brand. As we continue to build the Luxe Hotels brand, we must keep our focus on providing genuine hospitality. The goal is to offer a home away from home that guests want to visit again and again.

As of this writing, we are growing the Luxe Hotels brand in Europe. The Luxe Rose Garden Hotel in Rome is our first site outside of the United States. It is located across the street from the US Embassy, one block from Rome's most renowned street, Via Veneto. The elegant hotel hosting sixty-five rooms and suites, featuring a mix of contemporary and classic décor, with eleven-foot ceilings, a great bar, and a great indoor pool and sauna. At the front desk, guests will find the most welcoming and caring team who will guide them to the hidden local restaurants, attractions, and the best tour guides in the city, which makes the difference for anyone's visit to this magical city.

The owner of the hotel, Alessando Lucio Massari, said, "The Rose Garden Palace is the creation of my father Lucio. He worked all his life to achieve this result. With my father's friendship with Mario Perillo, one of the travel industry's great men, they were able to open the Rose Garden Palace in one of Rome's best locations." Alessandro and his wife, Tetyana, really care for their hotel and the guest experience that they provide.

ULTIMATE BRANDING AND MARKETING

Gene Simmons of the outrageous rock 'n' roll band KISS, of all people, has confirmed to me the importance of building integrity in a brand, and ensuring its success and appeal. In 2003, Gene became a good friend when he was filming his *Family Jewels* TV series at both Sunset and Rodeo hotel.

My daughter saw him in our restaurant at the Luxe Sunset. I was carrying her on my shoulders, and he overheard her as she said to me, "Aba, that man has such pretty hair."

Hearing that, Gene turned around and said, "I like your daughter! She is a very smart girl."

From there, we developed a friendship. At one point, he invited me to his home and showed me his incredible collection of products that carry the KISS branding: from records, to T-shirts, to PEZ dispensers. His branding machine is unbelievable. After the licensing tour at his beautiful home, he sat me down in his study and began showing me a video of a Rolling Stones concert and then a KISS concert. Both videos were shot in the same arena from the same exact angle and camera. He rewound the video and said, "Look carefully at the Rolling Stones concert," calling my attention to the fact that the audience members were older, lacking hair or having bald spots. Then he fast-forwarded to the KISS concert. The audience had full heads of hair, they were predominantly young people, sixteen- to thirty-year-olds, plus a healthy mixture of all age groups. He explained that marketing had been the real driver in coming up with the idea of painting the band's faces. Audiences don't know that there's a big age difference. Younger listeners focus on the sound and the music, not the ages of the performers. He said that he still packs sellout concerts all over the world wherever KISS performs. Gene Simmons impressed me with his vast knowledge and his insistence on the fact that "licensing and branding is where it is at in business for the long run."

It was an honor to be invited to his home, and eventually to his wedding. (Not everyone realizes that Gene is Israeli. He attended religious school in Brooklyn.)

I have to agree entirely with what Gene Simmons says concerning branding: "Branding is where it is at in this business, and all the investments one makes in that business to develop the brand, make that brand stronger, allowing it to live forever." That is where the revenues are because, in the case of Luxe, revenues tell you that the quality, graciousness, and elegance we offer is valued and important to people.

It's why guests continue to identify with the magic of the Luxe brand, and that's why people return to Luxe Hotels.

TALENT IS NOT ENOUGH—IT MUST BE MARKETED

Joshua Bell, a world-famous violinist who has performed with the world's best orchestras and conductors, agreed to participate in a 2007 study for *The Washington Post*. Joshua wore a baseball cap and played his usual repertoire using his $3.5 million violin. He played outside the metro subway station in Le Enfant Plaza in Washington, DC. There was a hidden camera videotaping the experiment. Approximately 1,000 people passed by Bell, only seven stopped to listen and four of those were children. He collected thirty dollars in tips from passersby. Two days before the experiment he sold out in the theater in Boston at an average of one hundred dollars a seat.

This experiment pointed out to me the significance of marketing. Talent is not enough on its own. If the talent is not marketed, you cannot succeed. Effective marketing is key to expose any and all products and services any entity offers. No matter how great the product is, it always needs to be marketed.

ALL THAT YOU WANT, MORE THAN YOU EXPECT

If our goal is to exceed our guests' expectations, we must go beyond having "satisfied guests." They need to be wowed. They need to feel special to be guests for life. To achieve this goal, we as a team must provide extraordinary service at every touch point.

After booking a hotel room, the first individuals to engage our guests are the valet and bellman. We pay special attention to these individuals at our front line. The more information and knowledge they relay to our guests—the better the guest experience.

Every member of our staff makes a difference in creating an emotional connection with our guests. They are each a link in our Luxe Hotels chain of excellence. If one link breaks, the entire chain falls apart.

What we want to deliver to our guests is "all that they want, and more than they expect." Every Luxe employee strives to deliver that to every one of our guests.

WE ARE CUSTOMER-CENTRIC

An old friend from Australia recently called me to tell me a story. He had attended a pharmaceutical conference in Sydney at the Hilton Hotel, with over 1,000 attendees. A human resource culture trainer came up to speak. She opened her presentation by telling the entire crowd about her recent visit to Los Angeles, where she was attending another conference. She described a painful flight to LA that had started off with delays in Sydney, and then had to wait on the LAX tarmac for hours. Then the airline lost her suitcase containing all her clothes that she was planning to wear to the conference. She usually stayed at hotels near the airport, but her corporate travel agency booked her at the Luxe Hotel on Sunset. After experiencing these delays and mishaps, she was very frustrated and apprehensive going to a hotel she had not been familiar with.

She then went on to describe how from the minute she arrived at the hotel, it seemed as though she landed on an island and could not believe the beautiful lush landscape and serene environment. She was met by the welcoming valet attendants. As she walked into the lobby, she was welcomed by the front desk team. She explained to them that the airline lost her baggage. Hudith, the front desk manager, immediately offered her a car to take her shopping to buy clothing that she would need to wear for the next few days. She could not believe the care and genuine thoughtfulness that each person she met displayed.

After shopping and eating in our restaurant, she went to her room and continued to mention the welcoming eyes of the housekeepers and other hotel employees that she came across. She told the conference audience that she felt at home and cared for. She knew she was in the right place. At the end of her recalling the details of her stay with us, she said, "We in the pharmaceutical world must learn from this hospitality industry example how to take care of our own clients." This is what we do. We treat every guest as an individual. Each guest has their own story and we take care of them and their personal world. This is why we call ourselves "customer-centric."

I rely on my staff to create that positive experience. We honor the employees who go above and beyond the call of duty by thanking them for their work and recognizing their excellent service through internal programs that we have developed. We lead by example and I want the Luxe Hotels to be the personification of my philosophies as to what true hospitality is all about.

HONOR YOUR PROMISE

The absolute worst thing we could do is tell a guest we would do something, like deliver something to the room—such as extra towels, robe, razor, or toothbrush—and not do it. We began a "Promise Log" by the phone operator's desk where we log in the time "promised" and what the item was to be delivered to the room. We call the room to ensure that the task was performed.

Our property management system that checks guests in also has the capacity of storing guests' profiles on the screen as they check in. We make certain that we enter all of the likes, dislikes, or other relevant information. Our team members are encouraged to let the guests know upon check-in, for example, that extra towels were already placed into the room, or confirm that the pot of coffee and croissant will be delivered at 6:45 a.m. the next morning—as they like it.

Providing clean and comfortable rooms at competitive rates is not enough—it's the bare minimum. For guests to return, we need to create lasting impressions. Every individual in the hotel must be focused on making each guest experience a special and memorable one. We have an opportunity to have a guest for life when we turn a negative experience around. Things will always happen, no matter how prepared you and your property are in anticipation of guests' needs. It is how you handle an issue or a problem that will make the difference for your guests. They will not always remember what went wrong, but they will remember how a hotel handles it.

I also encourage my team to inquire with our guests, to see if they are satisfied with every interaction, from the point of their arrival to their checkout. We need to know if there any issues to be addressed. The goal is to correct problems immediately to ensure our guests are experiencing excellence throughout the hotel. If a guest is dissatisfied with our service, they may not complete a comment card or even write a bad review. They will make a mental decision not to return to our property.

At Luxe Hotels, a significant part of our training is *conflict resolution*. We train our employees on different methods of actively listening to our guests with genuine empathy, giving them a chance to talk through their complaint without interruption. We then find different ways to defuse the situation, genuinely and sincerely apologize, and quickly find a satisfactory resolution. We should never lose our patience or get defensive because this will further agitate the situation and our guest. We have found that this methodology has resolved many issues in a timely and effective manner.

I recently overheard a desperate guest telling one of my front desk employees that he was extremely disappointed to learn that the Getty Museum was closed. He had promised his wife a visit to the museum on a Monday prior to their late-night flight. Rather than saying,

"Sorry, I can't help you," she said, "You know, the owner of this hotel just told me about this wonderful home museum only ten minutes from here, called The Frederick Weisman Museum. Should I try to get you into the 10:30 a.m. tour?" The couple was so ecstatic about the museum, they tipped the helpful front desk for arranging an unforgettable experience for them. That is what we call "true" Luxe service.

ENCOURAGEMENT FROM RONALD REAGAN

Meeting former president Ronald Reagan on several occasions had a very positive impact on me, as it was an honor to meet him. How this relationship with the former president started was an unforgettable experience. I received a call to my home at about 9:00 p.m. one evening. It was a director of sales from another beautiful hotel in Los Angeles. She apologized for calling me so late at night. She said, "President Reagan and Nancy had a birthday party at Chasen's Restaurant, in Beverly Hills. At the party, one of the president's dear friend's wallets disappeared, and they decided to handle all the details and card replacements the next day. The president is asking if you could arrange a complimentary room for his friend tonight at Rodeo Drive."

Confused, I asked Roselyn why she wasn't taking care of this request in her hotel, and she said that her general manager would not accommodate complimentary accommodations. She had heard about my reputation and knew that I would step up.

I thought for a moment and replied, "Yes, I will accommodate President Reagan's request." It would be my honor to help such an important guest.

Roselyn responded, saying, "In exchange, Mr. Reagan would love you to come to his office tomorrow morning to meet with him, and you can bring a guest." I invited my banker who has now been a friend for many years, Jacqueline Harrell, from Bank of California, to join us.

The next day, we went to meet with President Reagan. We sat and talked with him, and he proudly showed us his office in The Fox Towers in Century City. He pointed out the many hand-carved chess sets he had been given as presents along with photographs around his office. We got to his desk and I noticed a quote engraved on a plaque that said, "There is no limit to what a man can do or where he can go if he does not mind who gets the credit." I feel that this quote portrays the root to the success of any company.

As we sat down on President Reagan's couch, he said to me, "Mr. Harkham, my staff says that your company is all about relationships."

"Yes sir," I replied, "this is what my team and I aspire to continuously develop, genuine relationships."

He said, "All of my relationships, and all of my friendships, and all of my dealings are important to me. Although I am no longer the president, I still talk to Margaret Thatcher at 10:00 a.m. every Tuesday. It's my way of keeping in touch."

The president was sincere, and I felt that he enjoyed speaking with us. He felt at ease with me and he had inquired about me via Roselyn. He knew the Luxe Sunset Boulevard Hotel. He mentioned that he'd been there as governor when the property was still The Bel Air Sands Hotel. The entire experience of meeting with him was incredible.

A few months after our meeting, President Reagan's staff and my team arranged for him to have lunch with me at the Luxe Sunset Boulevard Hotel. This too was a very moving experience. During the meal, he talked about the importance of the people with whom you surround yourself, and he said that he always selected people smarter than himself.

"The problem with business people," he said, "is that their egos don't let them hire people that are smarter than they are."

"Smart people can make you grow faster." He said, "I feel sorry for people who get intimidated when they are around smarter people than themselves."

Our vice president of sales knew that President Reagan really liked freshly baked chocolate chip cookies. So, our executive chef brought out a variety of cookies on a platter and placed it in the middle of the table. The president stopped talking and just sat there looking at the cookies. I thought, "Oh no, is there a problem with the cookies?"

His two security guards were right there on either side of him, and finally one of them broke the silence and said, "Mr. President, Nancy is not here. You can have a chocolate chip cookie."

So, he smiled and said, "No. I was just looking for the one with the most chocolate chips."

With that, he picked one up and began to thoroughly enjoy eating it. I was so pleased to have given him that little pleasure. After all, that is what true hospitality is all about: the little things.

As he was leaving the hotel at the conclusion of our lunch, he walked up to a group of people that were checking into the hotel and he introduced himself to them. He had noticed them watching him. He began shaking their hands and hugging our arriving guests. "Oh my God: President Reagan!" one of them yelled out.

"How are you, my dear?" he asked her. "Where are you from?"

"Arizona."

"I love Arizona," he said, and he hugged her.

"Oh my God," the woman gushed with tears.

Then he went to the folks next to her and he hugged them, too. It was truly something spectacular to observe. He was just so normal, so kind, so generous.

There was a story about President Reagan that was told to me by a friend. Whenever Marine One helicopter landed at the White House, there were always Marines stationed there to salute him. After several months of saluting, he noticed there was usually the same uniformed African American soldier holding a US flag in his hands. On one particular day, the president arrived at the White

House and after excusing himself, he walked up to the soldier and said, "The way you hold that flag makes me so proud to be an American. I wanted you to know that. What is your name?" He told him his name and the president shook his hand and said, "It's a pleasure to know you."

The soldier stood there and took all of this in and he had a beautiful expression of appreciation that everyone who had witnessed this incident will never forget.

Hearing President Reagan's advice was definitely one of the highlights of years past. I learned a deeper meaning of the word "kindness" and that we must always put our egos in check and look to hire people brighter and smarter than we are.

ASSEMBLE AN "A" TEAM

Assembling a great team is critical. A team must also share your vision. Hiring the right person has been important at every stage of my career. There are no shortcuts to creating the "A" Team. As I am getting older, I see the power of doing this. Assembling that team is a top priority.

My ritual when I go to my hotels is to make the rounds to say "hello" to the teams in housekeeping, laundry, kitchen, restaurant, front desk, catering, and valet to see if everyone is well that day. This makes it personal for me, and my employees feel I am present. Even though I was an extremely young entrepreneur, I realized early on that no act as a leader is trivial. Every action and word has an impact. I always want to operate credibly.

I also believe education is key. People should not have to execute the daily responsibilities of working without pausing now and then for a reception or gathering where appreciation is shown. At our employee events, I like to share new discoveries about the service industry. I also like to share a bit of inspiration and relaxation as well.

The great-grandson of Sir Winston Churchill recently stayed at the Luxe Sunset Boulevard Hotel. He gave me a copy of his book, *God & Churchill*, where he wrote the following inscription, "Having just seen your thirty-year celebration video in the room, I was very impressed that your leadership philosophy mirrors my grandfather's, especially in recognizing team efforts. I hope you enjoy this, my first book on my great-grandfather: *God & Churchill*. Lead like Churchill. Courage, Faith and Integrity. Warmest regards, Jonathan Sandys." This inscription means so much to me. I'm always grateful to receive unsolicited positive feedback about our staff from people who have stayed at my hotels.

As leader of my organization, my job is to do everything possible to bring out the best in each member of our team. Everyone must do his or her job to seek and achieve his or her own personal best for our company, in order to make it as good as it can be. In other words, I need each employee to reach 100 percent of their potential to serve the company as a whole. We want to create an environment of achievers, striving to reach 100 percent of each team member's potential. It becomes a force with exponential power and productivity.

The late, great coach John Wooden once said, "To win championships you have to find the right players for the necessary roles, then let them focus on what they do best." Business is like that too.

My staff is not just a random collection of people who show up every day. Our company, standards, and values are like a magnet. We attract the best of people. It matters to me, and obviously, it matters to all of them. That's been the basis of my entire working career. I want my employees to have the feeling that they "don't just work here," but rather "like they own the place." Another notion I talk a lot about is the concept of "happiness." If something is bothering a member of the staff, they cannot concentrate on their job. Happiness is a big deal. There is no stopping a happy employee. If there are unresolved issues, it will prevent that employee from reaching his or her full potential. If my employees are at peace, they will be open and be able to be genuine.

I truly have love in my heart for people who work with me, whom I regard as my extended family. Building allegiance and loyalty is very important. As a team, we are all part of something bigger. I tell my team they are the "other half" of me. I could never do it without my team.

I, like other general business owners—and in particular hotel owners—expect a minimum of 10 percent to 12 percent net returns from my investments. However, the goal is always to achieve this level of return without sacrificing service.

It's not easy to achieve this objective, because the hotel business is one of the most volatile and vulnerable industries. When the economy reacts, or if any unforeseen disasters occur, hotels are one of the first businesses to be affected. Hotels can empty overnight.

Assembling an "A" Team is critical and is an ongoing process. Like all businesses, hiring the best people who share your vision and enthusiasm to grow and constantly achieve excellence are crucial to a company's success, and there are no shortcuts building an effective "A" Team. It is like fighting a war. You can't win a war until you have effective, well-armed "boots on the ground." The team needs to be out there constantly delivering hospitality excellence.

As leader of my organization, it is my job to do everything possible to bring out the best in every individual member of our team. Passion and care are elements that I want from my team, and I am happy to say that I have it. I found an industry that I love, and I want to communicate that kind of passion, both directly and through my team. Whatever I do, I want to do it 100 percent.

ACKNOWLEDGE AND APPRECIATE

I remember an instance on one of my trips to Japan, when I had purchased some beautiful, but very heavy glass antique vases in London.

When I got to my hotel in Tokyo, the bellboy carried up the rather heavy luggage. When we arrived at my room, I handed him the equivalent of five dollars because he well deserved it. He would not accept the money.

I asked, "Why not?"

He explained, "We aren't allowed to take money from guests; we are here to take care of you."

We entered the room, and he placed all my bags in places where I could get easy access to them. Again, I tried to tip him for his effective and efficient service, and again he declined accepting it.

Finally, I folded the cash, and put it in his suit pocket. He thanked me profusely and then he took it out of his pocket, placed it on the television, and walked out. I thought, *Wow, that is the definition of elegant and sincere service.* That episode really made an impression on me.

I love the hospitality business because it provides so many opportunities to express appreciation to our clients and employees. It is so important that everyone on the team feels needed and appreciated, and by having an open dialogue, everyone on the team is supported, focused, and happy, and they pass on their happiness to the guests.

I've been told by guests again and again, "You and your staff make us feel so special at your hotels." If they are individuals familiar with the Old Testament, they say, "I feel that it is the spirit of Abraham embodied in you."

I've studied the story of Abraham and his tent, open on all four sides, but the more I read about the man whose greatest happiness was to welcome people into his world, the more it makes me want to create an exquisite and meaningful experience for people. I do whatever I can to teach this concept to my staff.

Another experience I had years ago demonstrated to me how I wanted my team to conduct themselves when given a situation that is based on immediate and proper conflict resolution. While staying at a Sheraton Hotel in Nassau, Bahamas, I was robbed in my room. The thieves took my cash, but thankfully left my credit cards. I went to report the theft at the front desk.

The desk clerk's reply was: "Talk to our insurance company, sir. Here is their phone number. We are not responsible for that."

I said, "Fine. No problem." And then I went out and replenished my wallet with cash.

The next day, I was robbed again. And that's where the real problems began. I went down to the front desk again and told the desk clerk what had happened. I felt that I shouldn't have to pay for my last night at the hotel because of this experience. When I expressed my displeasure, without my knowledge they called the police, and three detectives showed up within a few minutes. They literally handcuffed me for "attempting to walk out on my bill." I guess they thought I was some sort of a con man. The whole situation was a nightmare.

The woman at the front desk could have avoided all that craziness and loss for Sheraton with a different attitude. I sued them and successfully won the case.

A PROUD RECOGNITION

While my natural instinct is to remain modest and keep on working, there are several people in my life who have publicly honored me recently, which has caused me to begin to accept, acknowledge, and appreciate my own success. I am humbled to hear these people calling my achievements and me "a great business success." I find myself arguing back about how I still don't feel that I have achieved all my goals. Perhaps that is because I see myself as still being in the middle of my career, and still a far cry from being able to rest on my laurels. I can now say from personal experience that accepting our own success is often difficult. Here is an example of one the humbling honors recently bestowed upon me.

In June 2018, I hosted an employee recognition luncheon for my staff and select members of my family at The Luxe Sunset Boulevard Hotel. I was happy and proud to give thanks to my employees for the great job they have been doing. At this luncheon, my guests included every department of the hotel, along with my 103-year-old father and my older brother Terry, who was on a visit to Los Angeles.

I stood up to address the staff, and after I was finished speaking, my brother Terry asked for the microphone, explaining how he wanted to say something to the gathering as well. The first thought that went through my head was, *Terry, what on earth are you going to say?*

I couldn't imagine what he wanted to address to the members of this gathering.

Terry took the microphone and spoke in a very sincere and conversational voice to my staff and employees. I sat there stunned and genuinely touched to hear Terry telling everyone how proud he was of me. He proceeded to eloquently tell everyone about how I had worked hard for years for all the success that I have achieved in my years as a hotelier.

Listening to Terry made me recall how, at the time I embarked upon the hotel business, I honestly thought I would be a failure. As I look at it now, these feelings of inadequacy were embedded in me because I thought my father didn't believe in me when I was growing up, and my teachers sadly only confirmed my shortcomings. Looking back on my childhood hurts and resentments, I now realize that my father's lack of attention toward me wasn't aimed at me personally; it was merely a case of my father simply not having the time to devote to me. I have harbored these feelings of hurt and emotional neglect all my life.

However, at that luncheon, to see the look on my father's face, I knew that I had finally arrived at a point where I have earned and achieved his both approval and pride. The smile on my father's face that afternoon while Terry spoke confirmed to me that my dad truly did believe in me. I have so much to be thankful for in my career as a hotelier.

HOSPITALITY IS CONTAGIOUS

One of the things that makes me happy is that I am also receiving incredible feedback from people who come to stay at my hotels. I recently received a letter from a woman who had arrived at one of my Luxe Hotels suffering from an enormous head cold. My employees in the lobby all instantly noted this, and they were concerned for her well-being.

The woman checked in at the front desk, and she was escorted to her room with the bellman transporting her bags. Within the hour, she received a knock on the door, and was told it was room service. The startled woman tried to explain that she had not ordered anything from room service.

However, the server at the door politely explained, "Madame, this is a bowl of freshly made chicken soup for you. We want to make certain you take care of yourself and get well. The soup is complimentary."

In the highly appreciative letter that she wrote to me, she told me of how horrible she had felt when she arrived. She then went on to explain how that one act of kindness from my staff had completely and genuinely changed her entire outlook on her stay.

That made me proud of my staff's high level of excellence and proud of myself for having instilled in them such a sense of giving and gracious service. Reading her unsolicited letter made me so happy. This is what ensures guests will return and become loyal clients.

I decided long ago that if ever I were to build a hotel brand, it would have to be up to my high standards with my own trademark brand of excellence in hospitality. My goal was to have a brand where people not only get everything they desire, they get more than they anticipated. Our guests are shown appreciation and a welcoming smile by every one of my employees, from the minute they enter the hotel. I have set the tone for unsurpassed hospitality, and my staff has fully embraced my welcoming standards.

Chapter 9
WINE IS IN OUR CULTURE

HARKHAM WINES

At the beginning of 2005, two partners and I bought a winery in Australia, which would become Harkham Wines. Originally, we bought it for the real estate. We completed the purchase in February, which coincides with the vintage time, the period when grapes are ripe and ready to be picked and processed into wine.

We contracted the former owner to stay on for the first three months of the changeover. He had picked a small number of grapes from our vineyard to make wine in his own "show winery."

My two partners were my brother Terry and his son, Richie. We decided to go to the winery to help the vintner, and we liked it so much, we saw an opportunity to expand its reach. The thing that attracted us was the allure of taking something natural, like grapes, and turning them into something so amazing, like wine. There is a real challenge to wine-making that attracts us to the industry. Just as the weather is never the same two years in a row, no wine will ever be the same two years in a row. Every year, there are new challenges.

Harkham Wines is in Hunter Valley, the oldest wine region in Sydney, Australia. We are one of the most unique wineries in the world, and the only fully committed kosher winery in all of Australia and Asia. We also make natural wines, which are 100 percent grape juice. That means no chemicals, no preservatives, and no additives. It is just 100 percent fermented grape juice.

Wine is in our heritage and our background. My mother, Aziza, used to make this style of natural wine for our family in the 1950s in Israel, with no electricity or running water. She used to pick grapes and make wine. Today our most famous wine brand is made in her honor. It is called "Aziza's," which we named for her in 2009.

MAKE IT KOSHER

The winery was not kosher when we purchased it. To figure out how to make that transition, we visited with the Chief Rabbi of Israel, Rabbi Mordechai Eliyahu. When the formalities were out of the way, the Rabbi turned to Richie and asked him, "So what do you do?"

My nephew Richie replied, "I make wine."

The rabbi asked, "Is it kosher?"

"No," said Richie.

And he said, "You have to make the wine kosher!"

Richie replied, "We are having a hard enough time making wine, let alone kosher wine."

Then the rabbi said to him, "If you make kosher wine, you will have the most successful kosher wine in the whole world."

He then proceeded to ask, "Imagine, for every single person who drinks a glass of your wine, you will get a blessing from their drinking that glass of wine."

Now we produce some of the highest quality kosher wine in the world. We sell out every year. Our flagship wine is consistently the Aziza's Shiraz and Chardonnay.

The wine is sold in many great restaurants in Australia, including Icebergs, Bentley Bar, Brae, and Quay. We sell out to the restaurants in a single day. It's also sold internationally at some of the best restaurants, including Noma, regarded as the number one restaurant in the world, which opened in Sydney in 2015. We were one of the few wines to make it into that restaurant. We sell a lot in New York, at some of the city's most famous restaurants. We also sell our wine at the Luxe Hotels on Sunset and Rodeo Drive. It can also be found at the best wine shops in the world, including Paris and Hong Kong.

Wine is in our culture. We want to capture everything that happens in nature in that bottle: all the rain, all the sunshine, and nothing else. Every time you add something else to it, you would lose one of those natural characteristics. Presently, Harkham Wines is also one of the top ten cult wine brands in Australia. Our goal is to be number one, and we're getting there.

I go to Australia every year around harvest time to help pick the grapes and make the wine. As a brand, we really feel like we are making a difference in the wine world in two ways. First, kosher wine has a really bad reputation. All the kosher wine in America—or at least 90 percent of it—is boiled. We don't boil our wines. Second, 95 percent of our wines are consumed by non-Jewish people who don't care whether or not it is kosher.

In regard to the art of winemaking, we go back to nature and the old-fashioned way that people used to make wine. We've made a big stir in the Hunter Valley. Our future in this realm is looking very bright for us. I'm proud to say the most well-known wine writers from some of the most esteemed publications in the world are constantly writing about the Harkham Winery: *The Sydney Morning Herald*, *The New York Times*, *Fine Wines of the World*, *Good Living*, and *Jane's Holiday Wine Companion*—an Australian newspaper.

PILLAR THREE
SETTLING DOWN & PARENTING

"Our deepest human need is to be cared about and to be connected."

—Dennis Praeger

Chapter 10
FINDING LOVE

MARRIAGE

As I approached the age of thirty-five, I thought I was ready to start thinking about marriage. Growing up, my father constantly communicated to all of us five boys that we should not consider marriage until we were at least thirty-five. I was the only one who listened, though. I quickly learned that the skills that were successful in my business life did not seem to work so well in my marriage.

I was conscious of my thirty-five-year-old goal to settle down and start the process of working on a healthy marriage and raising a family. The garment industry was a hectic environment with endless deadlines for designing, producing, and shipping merchandise to clients for every season. The added pressures to present the new seasons' fashion collections were beginning to burn me out. The perfectionist in me had to have each new season's collection look better than the last. New and fresh collections were the reason clients increased the size of their orders season after season. I needed to get off this merry-go-round.

I was extremely conflicted about leaving a successful business, but I knew this was the right decision for my life at the time. I said, "no more" and I decided to move on. At this time Jonathan Martin was very successful with annual sales in excess of fifty million dollars a year and I was proud to have been an integral part of building the company.

Six months after leaving Jonathan Martin, I went sailing at Turnberry Isle in Florida at the invitation of my LA stockbroker, Jeff Levy. Jeff was celebrating his birthday with twelve of his friends and clients. It was a beautiful, lavish hundred-foot super-yacht and to me, it was an unforgettable charter. The captain and staff were on board serving food and lots of alcohol. Jeff had done well that year and was celebrating.

During the sail, I struck up a conversation with Ken Leven, a mortgage broker from LA. One of the many topics we discussed was home mortgages. I mentioned that I owned two homes in Beverly Hills, free and clear with no mortgage. Ken almost choked on his drink and said that was crazy. For tax write-off purposes and a bunch of other reasons, he introduced me to Carol, a great loan broker in Brentwood.

Within ninety days, Carol, through her contacts, arranged a loan for both my homes on Foothill Drive in Beverly Hills.

I felt a personal need to meet Carol and express my gratitude for making the loan process so easy and pleasant. During lunch Carol asked me if I was dating anyone at the time. She said there was a very special girl that worked in her office as a loan processor whom she wanted me to meet. After hearing Carol's intriguing description of her, I asked if she was Jewish and she answered affirmatively.

I was excited to meet her. In fact, I called her the same evening and asked her out for dinner the following night. She accepted. Out of respect for her privacy, I will refer to her as "Karla."

Karla and I were smitten with each other from the first date. After dating for four months, we were ready to commit to marriage. She was twenty-five and I was thirty-five. Within nine months, she would become my fiancé.

During the time that we were courting, I encouraged her to attend a meditation retreat with my favorite teacher in the California desert. She attended and enjoyed it but was not wowed by it. She expressed that she preferred our Jewish traditions. From that, we eventually agreed to pursue a Jewish life and raise our children according to the Jewish faith. In the coming years, Karla and I were blessed with having three wonderful children, who continue to matter most in my life.

However, in our relationship, Karla and I hit some roadblocks; ones that after time proved to be insurmountable. I believe a major factor that worked to the detriment of my marriage were emotions that I repressed as a child. Those emotions began to show their impact on me in my adult life.

As a child, I witnessed my parents having arguments, like most parents do. Unfortunately, my mom did not defend herself well with words and her actions. Instead she used her eyes and face to express the pain she was suffering. Witnessing these arguments left me with feelings of fear, anger, and insecurity. However, my anger was stuffed and stuck deep within me. I did not face this anger and I did not figure out a way to manage it.

This anger and insecurity traveled with me into my adulthood. In all my relationships with women, I was always preoccupied with their facial expression. *Did they look mad, sad, scared, or glad?* Depending on the response I got from the woman, it would determine if she was satisfied with me or not. I was desperately attempting to avoid any sort of conflict, and so I followed the pattern that I saw and learned from my parents' marriage. Carrying over these learned behaviors did not help me in making my marriage to Karla a success.

I was determined to always have a positive face in front of the kids and shield them from witnessing any problems that were appearing in my marriage. From dawn to late at night, my routine was to pray, work, learn, meditate, jog, and practice yoga. In this way, I was able to ground myself and remain positive for the kids.

I found that while I was able to say "no" without a problem in business, I could not do so in my marriage. I became a "yes" person to all of Karla's requests and needs. I was overly desperate to please her and to avoid any visible negativity between us. I lost the little self-confidence I had, and in the process, I lost all sense of my needs.

I also believe Karla lost respect for me for being this way. I needed to be stronger, firmer, and tougher in my marriage but still sensitive and diplomatic. It was a tough line to negotiate.

Unfortunately, these issues were impossible for us to overcome and our relationship dissolved after eighteen years together. We truly gave the marriage a good shot. We tirelessly consulted with advisors and therapists. But we could no longer squeeze the round peg into the square hole. It just did not work from very early on in the relationship.

Separation and divorce is a grueling and difficult experience. It took Karla and me two difficult and long years to disentangle from each other financially. We were fortunate enough that a good mutual friend, Moise Hendeles, a non-practicing attorney, came to the rescue. He interpreted the legal mumbo-jumbo and brought common sense and wisdom to resolve the financial issue between us with little hassle.

Karla and I will always be connected via the children, but we also developed a better working relationship between us. Better than what we had in the marriage, and with more mutual respect. All the contention between us is gone and that makes for a happier life, for our children—Aron, Benjamin, and Natalie—and for Karla and me.

THOUGHTS ON RELATIONSHIPS AND MARRIAGE

Looking back, I recognize that I rushed into my romantic relationship with Karla. It would have been better to take our time, considering we were selecting a life partner. We should have taken time to just have fun and get to know each other before we made a long-term commitment. In hindsight, we should have enjoyed each other as a couple— sharing interests while the magic was still in the air, in which time we would have learned how well we are able to resolve a conflict as a couple. This advice applies to all relationships, whether it is with friends, business associates, or lovers. It's about knowing the person. The ability to overcome conflict predicts the success and longevity of the relationship.

I realized that because we were unable to resolve conflict in our relationship, our marriage did not have the proper tools it needed to survive or grow successfully. We were unable to overcome conflicts that were arising. This is now the predictor for the success of any of my relationships. If the inevitable hurdles become insurmountable as ours did, then it is not going to work. And it's okay to move on.

When forming romantic relationships, it's imperative that we search out a partner with whom we can resolve conflicts without feeling that anyone lost in the outcome. There is no shortage of conflict in our lifetime, but it is up to us how we handle it.

Additionally, we must remember that people evolve and change. When the infatuation dissipates and the idealizing period is over, reality becomes more apparent after seeing the ups and downs and how each of us deals with them. Either we successfully work through our differences and accept the other's emotional baggage, or we walk away.

A strong marriage occurs when two individuals join and maintain their own identity, while compromising to find a common ground that brings those two people together as one. In my marriage, I did not remain true to who I was as an individual, and I felt like I had lost that power of knowing myself in my marriage.

At first, I also found it difficult to admit that I was going to be a part of the 65 percent statistic of failed marriages in the US. The divorce rate is still growing, partially because children are repeating the behavior they learned from their parents. We need to model good behavior, in a safe, loving environment for our children. This is the only way to break the cycle.

Chapter 11
PARENTING

THE ART OF GOOD PARENTING

My children, Aron, Benjamin, and Natalie, are the most important beings in my life. I have a special relationship with each of them.

Parenting is not a job for the faint of heart. Since first becoming one, I struggled to be a good parent. I read books, went to classes, and sought advice from friends, family, and professionals.

Raising my children constantly reminds me of my own character flaws, primarily my selfishness and lack of patience. Above all, parenting has taught me that love can be a one-way street. I have struggled with this aspect all my life. However, despite all my shortcomings and mistakes, it looks like Karla and I did something right when we see what upright, good people our children have become.

As I get older, I am increasingly aware that time is really precious. Additionally, I have learned that my children have made me overall a better person. Good parenting has always been a priority for me, and I am proud whenever people ask me about my children. I've heard over and over, from many different sources, that the most important time we have is time spent with our children. I totally agree. I realized early on, the most effective way to discipline was by modeling good behavior. With my children, it was essential that I exercise self-control in the way I spoke, in the way I dressed, in my daily rituals, and in my choices of entertainment.

Too many times in my lifetime, I have had good friends and family members confide that their child just stopped talking to them for extended periods. I am certain that this would be a most painful experience for a parent. To be locked out of my children's lives for an extended period is unimaginable. I understood the gravity of my responsibility to be a good parent and to build a healthy home environment for my family, where children are not only safe but also strong.

It was my duty to mentor my children and it was my job to teach them to handle responsibility and to grow to become happy and successful people. As they grow older, they will make some major decisions that will alter their lives forever.

As a father, I want to instill them with values so that they will know who they are and will not be swayed by negative forces. My parenting process began prior to when my children were even born. I realized Karla also had a serious role to play in raising our children. Looking back up to today, I am grateful that we parent as a team.

PARENTAL ROLES

Karla and I respected each other's roles in raising our kids. We were each ready to assist the other when necessary. We both have unique characteristics that complemented each other when raising our children. Even when we were going through rough patches, I always made sure that I displayed respect and cooperation toward Karla, wanting the kids to act the same way toward her. I was always conscious of doing my utmost to never undermine her in front of the children.

I made a point to never contradict Karla in front of any of the children, or in front of anyone else.

Jewish men prior to and during their marriage are constantly reminded of the episode in the Bible where the patriarch Abraham and his wife Sarah are discussing the fate of their son, Isaac. God clearly tells Abraham that he must listen to Sarah and honor her. In the same way, I accepted that Karla managed the details of the running of our home; that as a mom she knew deep in her gut the way the kids should be raised.

Both Karla and I made a distinct effort to spend quality time with Aron, Ben, and Natalie. I took them to "mommy and me" sessions where I was the only daddy in these classes, when they were two to five years of age. I took note of how the teacher spoke and related to the children. I also enjoyed observing how my kids related to other children in the room.

I jogged regularly with my kids when they were in their strollers at home and on vacations. If they were awake in the stroller, I regularly stopped to point out an interesting tree, flower, or some aspect of nature. I wanted to instill in my children the importance of a daily exercise regimen and to appreciate the world and the nature around them.

I made an effort to set a living example for my children of the importance of healthy eating habits. I wanted them to learn to take care of their bodies and not take their life and health for granted. I wanted them to look up to me and realize I was strong, dependable, and able to protect them, whatever the circumstance.

A HEALTHY ENVIRONMENT

From day one of my being a parent, I was intent that my children would grow up in a peaceful, calm environment. Before they were even born, I set out to create a beautiful home atmosphere that my children will remember as a place of warmth, safety, and serenity. It is my hope that they will create a similar atmosphere for their families in the future.

My most vivid memory as a child up to the time that I left my parents' home in Sydney at the age of twenty-one is that the physical environment around all of our homes and gardens were unattended by the adults. Our small house in Petah Tikvah, Israel, had close to a dozen family members living in it, with a single small toilet in the house. As middle schoolers, my brother Terry and I took matters into our own hands and took care of this problem. We got basic drawings and instructions from a builder that was a family member. Using basic tools, we picked a spot in the garden and successfully dug out a foundation and erected an outhouse, toilet, and shower.

When we moved to Sydney, there was also a lack of attention by the adults in the house to make our homes inviting and comfortable for the family and our visitors. There were always incomplete jobs around the house, broken door handles, ripped screens, or taps that leaked and were unrepaired for the longest time.

When I started dating Karla, I was extremely happy to learn that she shared the same value of living in a beautiful physical environment and she actually studied interior design in college.

Knowing that I was going to be married by the age of thirty-five, I had certain important tasks to accomplish in order for my future life partner and myself to focus on developing a healthy family dynamic and not waste valuable time in the pursuit of the stuff necessary for a physically beautiful home.

SHAPING A CHILD'S IDENTITY

As children, we have little choice regarding our circumstances, and can be easily defined by our parents. As we all know, if parents withhold encouragement and love during these formative years, it can be extremely detrimental to the child. As parents, we must be aware of the needs and changes our children go through in order for them to grow and thrive. If children don't receive that encouragement, they are left without the ability to believe in themselves.

Good parents know that kids need to be dragged out of their comfort zone if they are going to achieve success, develop good values, and grow in character. Lack of parental support or guidance can become a defining factor for years to come. Children need structure, support, discipline, and encouragement in order to become strong, successful people.

At some point, though, we all need to take charge of our own lives. Some people find themselves jumping through other people's hoops all their lives. They never achieve their own goals if they don't stop it. I admit I have done that for a large part of my own life. I've gone through endless hoops, hoping that I will finally succeed in other eyes. Proving ourselves to our parents can be a lifelong, endless quest.

I am very fortunate in having successfully gotten out of that cycle because it is like a hypnotic trance that one goes into. We can't live within anyone else's bubble.

For me personally, I find that I have been shedding that parental mantle progressively. Every year drives it closer to home. What would it take for me to finally say that my father was proud of me? As my father has just reached his 104th birthday, I still wonder.

My children will always know how proud I am of them, even when they "burst my bubble" and grow into their own identities, which they are successfully formulating.

THE TEENAGE YEARS

I don't believe that we should sit out the teenage years and wait for kids to outgrow this stage in their life. Teenagers have too much time on their hands, and they need guidance as how to channel that time for a fruitful and fulfilling life. Youth is the most precious energy and time in a life, yet the most difficult to navigate. The energy, power, and will is like fire—it could be destructive or wasted without proper mentoring and guidance.

Occasionally, teenagers need to be rebuked for certain actions that they take. As parents, we need to give them support and guide them through difficulties. Rebuking plays an important role in life and if kids don't receive that when it's due, they will be doomed to stagnation and complacency.

Children need to be told when they are duly wrong; otherwise how could they know to do right? This can be done from a place of love rather than anger and disappointment.

Parents need to be vigilant and actively concerned about the values that children are being taught. The kids must get a balance regarding the values both at home and at school. Parents need to reinforce the moral compass for their children that will guide them for the rest of their lives because they are our future.

My goal as a dad is to assist in harnessing this powerful energy by providing them guidance for their physical, emotional, and mental well-being with constant guidance and advice early and throughout their high school years. They are our future.

SET BOUNDARIES AND LIMITATIONS

It's important to set limits and boundaries with our children so they grow up being able to think clearly, to be responsible, compassionate persons. In Hebrew, we call that *gevura*. Even Zen Buddhists use this word. It means "setting limits and boundaries for inner strength."

Constantly giving and lavishing too much kindness will spoil the child. After having my three children, I learned that children love their parents naturally, without reservation. It's natural. There have been all sorts of studies where even an abused child will still want their parent because of that unbreakable bond. Therefore, a parent should not fear having to set boundaries, or say "no" when appropriate.

Parents need to ensure that they are not enablers by allowing kids to be challenged to deal with reality. A perfect example of this can be found in the book *Codependent No More* by Melody Beattie, where the author says, "You cannot simultaneously draw boundaries and be responsible for the person's feelings." There is no drawing of boundaries without guilt.

Every person needs to determine what their boundaries are. People should know their boundaries, moral and ethical, and how far they can push the envelope in all facets of their lives.

I often tell my children, "In order for us to have a genuinely good time together, we need to be respectful and at peace with each other's company. However, your non-response to my phone messages or texts, by being always so busy with school or career, yet making time for your friends, causes hurt feelings and unnecessary resentment, and ultimately damages our relationship." Kids need to be reminded to show respect to their elders.

Divorced parents need to remember that our job as parents doesn't stop with the divorce. The mantra I was told by a mentor is that of all the gifts I could give my children, the most important is the power of self-control. I want them to know that they can feel powerful feelings and think at the same time! I regularly repeated to the kids and I always tell them, "You have the strength within you, and you need to realize that your future is in your control."

I learned I should not be the enforcer, but rather the teacher. If a child didn't like a decision I made and was obviously unhappy, I would say, "You don't always get to vote. I am your dad. I have to make decisions and they may seem bad to you." But I am following my job description as a dad.

When I separated from Karla, Natalie was only three years old. Whenever she was with me, Natalie kept saying endlessly, "I want to go see Mommy!" I devised a strategy. I would put on a very concerned face and behaved as if her request was important and genuine and said, "You would like me to turn back right now, and take you back to Mom, right?" I would stop and wait for her to respond and I would say in a compassionate voice, "Well, I can't, sweetie, because you are staying with me tonight." If Natalie felt that she was not understood and that I was not listening to her, she would turn off. She would look for other ways to feel good. I always want to know how her day went, what sort of things she did at school, what are the weekend plans, or if anyone is giving her a hard time.

Parents need to make an effort to know where their kids are at all times. Drugs and alcohol are a big part of our culture, and I can't have my kids fall down that rabbit hole. We need to remind kids that life is full of ups and downs. They need to realize their blessings and that there are resolutions and ways to cope with what life brings.

The easy way to be a parent is to say "yes" all the time, but that isn't always the best way. You can't forget that you are the parent, and not the child. You've got to be conscious of sometimes setting aside your own wants and needs and let them know who's pulling the strings and who is in charge.

WHAT GETS PRAISED GETS REPEATED

On one of our family vacations to Maui in Hawaii, we stayed in a hotel that highlighted their beautiful parrots. I asked the person who was showing off the parrots, "How do you teach parrots to do these complicated things?" His reply was, "Every time the parrot does what I expect, I reinforce the good behavior by giving it some food. When the bird does not do the right thing, I just don't do anything.

Eventually, the actions that get praised and positively reinforced are repeated, and the more I reinforce the correct behavior the more it gets repeated." I believe that this is a valuable technique to follow when parenting.

On many occasions, usually when I am overscheduled, I forget to take note of the good and positive things my children are doing, whether it is just being helpful around the house, sharing or going out of their way to help others, or excelling in school. I found that I am more likely to notice when they do something wrong. I have learned that children are quick learners and want to be noticed. Their instinct proudly says, "Look at me, aren't I amazing?" They are asking us, as parents, to notice their abilities. I encourage Natalie's interest in all extracurricular activities including ballet, hip-hop, gymnastics, and piano lessons. Exposure to the arts is very important to foster creativity in a child. We created charts and had colorful stars that we maintained daily, and we tallied at the end of the week. On a monthly basis we rewarded those achievements.

Parental expectations can be lethal for the development of a child. Alternatively, when the parent gives positive reinforcement, the child can truly learn to feel their self-worth from within. Not everyone is so lucky.

Children are so open and so trusting of their parents. Whatever the parent wants a child to be is what the child is likely to become. When a child's sense of self-worth is fully intact, they can go through negative experiences in life and not become bitter or discouraged. I was lucky that my mother constantly told me that I am "royalty," so that is how I have always seen myself. She told my other siblings that, too. We all believed her. For example, I make such an effort to let my daughter know how special, talented, and smart she is, and how proud I am of her. Kids need that positive reinforcement.

A father has to teach his children. He should teach them how to grow and handle responsibility. Before we know it, children are going to be adults, making some major decisions that will alter their lives forever. If these values are not instilled in them, they are going to be easily influenced by the outside world. So, parents need to begin the process in their infancy.

We need to encourage all the people in our lives, no matter what age they are. We do that for family, friends, employees and guests. We all need positive reinforcement. My two favorite words are: "Acknowledge and Appreciate." No one can ever get too much of either.

SET THE STANDARDS

Parents always hope they will be a person their children look up to and will be an example to emulate. I hope that by living my life the way I have chosen, I will instill the right values in my children to carry them into their adult lives.

Building on this idea, I am especially grateful to my brother Terry for the story he recounted when he was with my son Benjamin and me recently. Terry was saying how the woman who was our very first patternmaker, Mrs. Zalinka, was still in touch with him, and that she often asked how I am.

My son said to my brother, "I can't believe you two could work together as brothers."

Terry said, "Are you kidding me? When I first saw your dad at the factory, I didn't know what was going to happen tomorrow. I didn't know if I was closing down, or what to do next. Then your father walked in, and a light turned on! He took my samples out that same day—he didn't waste a day—and about four months after he was doing this, all these orders were coming. Remember, I told you that I was going to give you half of my company, Efrem? I told you I was going to give you 50 percent of my stock. And your dad said, 'But Terry, you realize there's so much potential for Lulu Fashions. You can make a fortune. This could be an incredible company, Terry. Are you sure you want to give up 50 percent of your company?'"

Terry completed his story: "I said to him, 'It's a pleasure to give it up to you. You are so dedicated, you are so focused, you are so good, and you work so hard.'"

I stood there thinking, *Thank God my twenty-one-year-old son is hearing this!*

My brother saw that spark, that *nous*, and that drive in me. It is about showing up. You have to work. You have to be out there. Terry said to Benjamin, "I wanted to give it to your dad, because he earned it. He worked it, and he gave it all that he had."

PARENTING NEVER ENDS

No matter how old your children get, the role as a parent never changes and never ends. I am so happy to still have my father at the age of 104. He continues to be one of the most important people in my life.

Recently, I had dinner with him. We just sat there, and I said, "You look good, Dad, you look good. I'm sorry you are in pain, but you look better than yesterday."

He smiled in reply.

I find that he is at peace. I said to him, "Do you want to watch some television? Aren't you bored?"

"Why would I want to waste my valuable time watching television?" he asked.

Then I asked him, "Do you need something? Do you need more money?"

"No," he said, "I don't need more money."

Any money that I do give him, he just gives away. He loves giving five- or ten-dollar bills to the grandkids when they come to visit.

I am no longer waiting for my dad's pat on the back. I am still missing that in my life, but I am fine with never receiving it, as well. There is limited time in life. Childhood is over and I am not waiting around for that encouragement. His smile is good enough for me. My dad was never a physical kind of guy, so I don't ever expect any of that kind of demonstration of emotion.

Parents are humans, and so are not perfect. But to a great extent they make us who we are, and we have to admit to that fact. I am thankful and very respectful of my children's feelings, because I have been on the other side of this emotional roller coaster.

In retrospect, I can see that my dad was under a lot of pressure to make sure his children did the best that we could, and to achieve as much as we could. He wanted us to get out of our disadvantaged situation in Israel so much that he drove us to demand the very best we could muster from ourselves.

Now that I look back at it, I can give up my childhood resentment and put it to rest. In a way, I am thankful to my dad for demanding so much of me. Although he seldom told me, "I am proud of you, Efrem," I know now that, in his own way, he is proud.

Making my father proud is still a large part of my life. My father's history in education is an impetus for my personal involvement in building schools in Burma and sponsoring schools when the opportunity presents itself. Our family sponsored the first GAON Academy in Los Angeles, The Harkham-GAON Academy. I know that it pleases him greatly. Education was and is the main focus of his life's work, so I know that passing education on to others pleases him greatly.

It pleases me to make my father happy. He has shown me that parenting never ends and has created awareness in me of the impact every word, every action, and every emotion will have on my own children.

I've done most of my parenting with a lack of self-confidence. My strong desire to be a good father drove my success.

In raising my own children, I have overcompensated to show a model of unconditional love and empathy at every stage of their lives. In the end, a parent's responsibility is to teach values such as honesty, empathy, and gratitude. It's also to motivate, encourage, and empower our kids to be comfortable in their own skin, and to provide the necessary tools for survival, success, health, and happiness.

My goal for my children is to continue the journey I have begun and go further than I did.

Chapter 12
REINFORCING VALUES

CULTURE OF HONESTY

Honesty is of primary importance to me, whether it is child to parent or parent to child. It's a two-way street. I would tell my children, "If you don't feel comfortable coming to my home, I'd rather you tell me the truth." I would ask my son if sometimes he really doesn't want to be with me to say so, and I would thank him for being honest with me. I would say, "I know why you don't want to talk to me. It's because you don't think I understand you." That was very effective.

As men grow, we become better fathers. I let my boys see the openness in me as time progresses. For example, I was completely open with my son by saying to him, "The truth is that I've always walked on eggshells with Mom and sometimes with you. I don't want to walk on eggshells anymore. Who do you walk on eggshells with? Is it a family member, a teacher, who?" When he opens up and tells me, I applaud his openness.

As my boys got older, I constantly communicated that we needed to have honesty in our relationship, always starting a new level of truth. I chose not to walk on those eggshells any more. I learned that it is very important to also let the boys speak the truth. I made a concerted effort not to talk them out of what they were feeling. As a parent, I needed to face the truth at every turn of their development, and to listen to them.

I struggled not to lecture to my kids. Lecturing is a mistake for communicating, especially with teenagers. I needed to teach the culture of truth. This is the way to reach them. I would say over and over, "I want to start a new culture of honesty with you."

When there was nothing to talk about, I had some ice-breakers. My father didn't speak enough to me. So, I made it a point to speak to the kids. The topics were not small talk. It's more effective to talk about topics that are emotional. I would make it a point to find reasons to compliment them and generally relate to them. They are so smart, and they know when you are not speaking from the heart. Unblocking the heart is a prerequisite to being a good parent. Otherwise, they will not open their heart to me. If I sense an unusual silence with a child, I would tell them to be open and honest about what is bothering them, even if they want to say they are angry with me.

Children need to have structure and to learn how to work within a budget. I let them know I will not allow them to spend money frivolously. When the boys started college, I asked them to keep track of every dollar they spent and evaluate at the end of the month to determine whether they were over or under budget. I would tell them to be up front with me, be straightforward.

I needed the stomach to rein it in when they would play one parent against the other. The "yes" parent becomes the hero, while doing an injustice to the child's growth. I learned it's okay to say "no." I learned not to fear saying "no." When I first became a parent, I didn't believe that a child could love a parent unconditionally and thought that by saying "no"

I would lose that love. I realized later that isn't true. Saying "no" for the good of the child is the only way to go. We can't say "yes" just because of how it makes us feel as parents, but rather only if it is the right thing to do. We can't be responsible for how the child feels. Every time I feel bad saying "no," I have to remember to let it go. I refused to become a "yes" parent, in spite of the twinge of wanting that child's love and the fear they will hate me. But they need to know it's about the principle.

BREATHE THROUGH IT, BABY!

Over twenty years ago, prior to the birth of our first-born, Aron, Karla and I attended a Lamaze pre-birthing training class. The training was with two other couples, both also first-time parents. Though we were friendly during class time, we didn't keep in touch. Fast forward twenty years: Neil, one of the expectant fathers-to-be who was in the class, reintroduced himself to me at a major hotel conference in Phoenix. While we were chatting, he reminded me of a funny incident that happened in that Lamaze class over twenty years ago.

Neil reminded me of this encounter: "The instructor was telling us about the uncomfortable and sometimes painful condition of the women. The instructor continued to explain that the 'coach' needed to hold her hand and make sure she was breathing properly. The instructor had a life size doll of a baby, for the demonstration, explaining what a woman's breathing should be like. We were all listening very intently. Then she asked, 'Does anyone have any questions so far?' You raised your hand saying, 'Sorry to interrupt, do we get to meet the coach?' There was a blank look on her face, as she said, 'You are the coach!'" Neil continued. "Looking shocked and slightly embarrassed you said, 'Oh my God! Are you kidding me? I am the coach??' We all just cracked up!"

When the time came, I did step up to the plate during the birthing process. I remember saying to Karla very calmly, "Just breathe through it, baby, just breathe through it. Everything is going to be OK."

I still use that phrase during other life experiences.

A perfect example is when my son, Aron, served in the Israel Defense for fifteen months after high school in LA. The army training, for various reasons, was a very difficult time for him. I kept telling him to "just breathe through it, it's going to be OK," and it was.

So, the Lamaze instructor's words about remaining calm and breathing through the difficult challenges of life totally work. I took what she said to heart, and I use the key phrase often. It's such good advice.

LOVING SOMETHING GREATER THAN THEMSELVES

I recognize that religion need not be part of the family culture. Our choice, given my background and long tradition of being Jewish, Karla and I decided that we wanted to include religion as part of our family. However, I never stuffed religion down anyone's throat. I wanted to leave enough room for them to make choices about the question of divine providence on their own and choose their own spiritual path.

I was aware that in the same way we were providing nourishment for our children's bodies with all the healthy foods we served them, their souls also needed nourishment. I remind them that it is God that has blessed our family with our success, that our efforts and hard work alone are not the reason for the success. I wanted to teach my kids that we need to help people around us.

This entailed teaching them to be charitable and good-hearted. I lived this example by exposing all my children from a very young age to performing charitable acts. For example, for several years, I arranged for Natalie and a few of her close friends from school to visit a nursing home. The girls and I brought smiles to the hundreds of sad and lonely elderly faces. We also bought and served delicious desserts from the best local bakery.

On one visit to the nursing home, my one-hundred-year-old neighbor, Len Aaron, the founder of Aaron Brothers art supply stores, joined us. Wearing his fancy cowboy hat and Texas medals, he got up on stage to introduce himself and tell stories of riding the rail on his trip to California from Wisconsin in the depression years, and how he started out in his business.

He began telling us how was riding a coal car through Montana. He said that he was so cold he got some straw and wood and started a small fire on the train to stay warm. As the fire suddenly got out of control, he jumped off the train. He continued telling jokes about himself and his life. At one point he said, "Efrem, please don't forget me and leave me here, since I think I am the oldest person here! I am so old I don't even buy green bananas anymore." It was so nice to see the residents laugh and have a lot of pleasure from this whole experience of meeting Len Aaron and the children. It was also an unforgettable moment for Natalie and me. Len has since passed away. May his memory live on, and may he rest in peace.

In order to ensure my children grow up with good values, they need to be dragged out of their comfort zone. I am adamant that my children "do the right thing." I find American culture lacking in providing this guidance. I am adamant that children write "thank you" notes for gifts received. Doing these things helps support the family as a whole and demands the best of children. Knowing that, by nature, kids are restless, I have had to fill their time with as much spiritual guidance in their life as possible. I was constantly scheming ways as to how to best lure them to do meaningful activities throughout their lives, from infancy to adulthood. I try to constantly create an environment around me that is focused on learning and searching for meaning in life. I find that I never stop reminding my children of the principles and value systems I live by.

DEFEAT ANGER

When anger becomes habitual, there are many anger management workshops and seminars offered. Anger causes a loss of control. When someone displays this frazzled behavior, it is difficult, if not impossible, to have a meaningful discussion. When in this state, individuals usually say things that may impact people's entire lives, and rarely does it lead to a good outcome. However, as a parent, there is a place for anger when raising a child.

Maimonides teaches, "If you need to act angry, you should remain inwardly calm." While it's easy to blame our children and others for our problems in life, often the problem lies within us. Anger and hot tempers without control are like cancers in personal relationships. When an individual is angry and out of control, they have no positive emotions, and no capacity to step into another person's world and feel empathy toward anyone. An uncontrolled display of anger can impact a child for life.

There are ways to defeat anger. Rabbi Sachs says, "Stop. Reflect. Refrain. Count to ten. Breathe deeply. Leave the room, if possible. Go for a walk alone. Meditate or vent your toxic feelings alone." Either we defeat Anger, or Anger defeats us. It's our choice.

A person who is not happy and not at peace with himself or herself will not be able to overlook even the smallest things and will be upset by everything. The smallest issues can turn into major issues and the ability to appreciate one's blessings will be lost. This is an important lesson for both the parent and the child. I discovered in my own behavior that insecurity can quickly lead to irritability and anger. When I am sure of myself, nothing external is going to negatively impact me.

RESOLVING CONFLICTS

At every stage of development, I got into the habit of reminding my children that they are good at solving problems. I empower them to believe that they are smart and that when they use their brains, they can resolve any situation. However, it helps a lot if they voice their opinions about their concerns. When I know what the problem is, I will be able to assist them in resolving the issue at hand. There is a solution to almost every conflict.

My hope is that my children will not become hysterical when dealing with difficulty in their life. I want them to know that they have the capacity to remain calm and think. It's important to understand that sometimes in life, we are served curveballs. I remind my children that nobody ever dies from a feeling; that we are able to tolerate the feeling, think, be responsible, and resolve the problem.

READING EXPANDS A CHILD'S MIND

I learned a valuable lesson about children's love of reading. We used to read different books side by side. To model good reading habits, I learned from an educational consultant that you need to read out loud the same book to your child while they read it at the same time. This fosters discussions and conversations about the book's subject matters, like love, kindness, loss, and rejection. The whole world opened for me as a parent as we became emotionally connected to the stories and it created wonderful conversations that continue to this day.

The power of reading not only affected my family life, but it also ran over into my hospitality business. I instituted a book program for guests arriving with children. Once they walk through a Luxe Hotel's doors, they are greeted with a red wagon that is wheeled out by our front desk staff with a selection of stuffed animals and books. The children are always so excited to choose an age-appropriate book ranging from coloring books to novels. The joy that is communicated by this gesture makes the family, in particular the child, feel overjoyed and cared for.

A perfect example of the importance of exposing children to reading is a program offered through the Boys & Girls Club. The kids from the Club are taken to the local book store to purchase $25 worth of books, not comic books, only story books. It's a wonderful program that many times provides children with the first book they ever owned. I am proud to say my friend, Marty Cooper, came up with this program which changes so many lives every year. It illustrates how we must all do our part.

We are also fortunate at Luxe Hotels to have partnered with Scholastic, the largest publisher of children's books. They send us a monthly supply of a variety of engaging books and the children really enjoy them. We love watching their faces light up at the surprise.

PILLAR FOUR
INSPIRATION

"Life is a quest for meaning."

—Viktor Frankl

Chapter 13
THE QUEST FOR MEANING

LOOKING FOR ANSWERS

By the time I was twenty-five, like so many others that age, I began questioning the basic elements of creation. How do you explain physical growth and change for plants and animals? How did the earth come to be? How do you account for sickness and disease? Overwhelmed by the sheer depth of these queries, I decided to put that quest aside when I came to realize that the mystery of life will never be fully explained because the human mind is finite and can only process information up to a point. Some things just don't need proving. It was a futile waste of time. I needed to go beyond the mind and reach for the soul.

REMAIN AUTHENTIC

At a relatively young age, I was blessed to experience great financial success. Being immersed in the business world from the age of eighteen, I learned I needed to be constantly responsible, particularly when ensuring I will not be taken advantage of by the multitude of self-centered and greedy sharks in every industry I worked in. I also felt that focusing my life only on work was going to lead me to an empty and boring life. I needed to back it up with an interpersonal spiritual component, and I realized there was a deeper meaning to my existence. Like a moth that seeks light, I had the same yearning to gaining more wisdom. I was absolutely not interested in the nightlife scene that was rampant in LA in the excessive 1980s.

Instead, I turned my back on partying and set off on a search for spiritual meaning. Until then, my personal spiritual road had been one with lots of twists and turns. Once I was no longer living with my parents, I was free to explore other religions and faiths. Oddly enough it led me from Judaism, to Buddhism, and then all the way back to the Judaic experience.

There are two ways of getting into the proverbial waters of spirituality. Either enter the water one toe at a time, or dive in head first. Like all other aspects of my life, I had to learn about this other aspect of existence. So, I began learning to meditate, began practicing yoga, and learned about Buddhism.

My ultimate goal was to strive to be more authentic. I wanted to stop wasting my life pretending to be other than what I really am. I strove to connect my exterior physical being to my interior world.

The word "personality" comes from the Greek word *persona*—meaning "mask." Over the years I have worn many masks—one for my parents, one for my siblings, and one for my employees and friends. It became a challenge keeping track of all the personas I put on. I contend with my masks every day in order to show my original face as best as I can. Wearing the mask creates unnecessary pressure on myself.

To this day I constantly work on removing the protective armor I used to protect myself from the harsh reality of the world. I work to recognize what is reality and what is not. This opens up my blinders to allow people and experiences to enter my life and create the long-lasting relationships and friendships that I know enhance my life. It is a constant task, yet one that I enjoy and look forward to on a daily basis.

LAUGHTER IS A MEDITATION

In the early stages of my spiritual search, I embraced Buddhism because it teaches you to still the mind. I had a void, and it was too great. It needed to be filled. Buddhism teaches you to do service (kind acts for others) without seeking a reward or acknowledgment. Its tenets emphasize the ecstasy of the heart (love, joy, sex, passion, prayer). It teaches silence—knowing when to shut up, and to be connected to others who are silent. When I silenced my mind, I began to see that my mind operated better, with more clarity.

Buddhism teaches that climbing your inner mountain makes a man out of you. It's not easy, but we must do it. It's about putting aside all fears.

In the midst of my quest, I went on a three-day retreat that changed the course of my life. I was introduced by an owner of an LA retail chain, Elizabeth, to a Zen organization called Jacumba, located near Barstow, California. The organization was subsidized by families in Beverly Hills and was located on a two-hundred-acre ranch. I loved going there for weekends to expand my mind, learn, celebrate, and meditate. It was really an enlightening and mentally freeing experience for me, having been working under intense focus and stress.

While at this retreat, I really got into the Buddhist lifestyle, and adopted a much-disciplined way of living. I participated in numerous meditations.

In a room with over one hundred people, we were instructed that for the next fifty-five minutes we would laugh nonstop, as loud or low as we wished and preferably with our eyes closed. We had to direct the laughter at funny situations that came to mind like a funny incident at work, an interaction with a family member, or an amusing story. The laughter came from a deep place, making light of serious and uptight situations. This allowed for a lot of tension to be released and was a cathartic experience.

After the exercise was complete, and we were all drenched with sweat, a small bell rang. For the next ten minutes, we were told to find a comfortable place on the carpeted floor and lie on the ground. After all that nonstop laughter it was time to switch gears; it was time to silence the brain for a few minutes.

I remember how clear I felt after this meditation. Rather suddenly, I had a wonderful realization. We can advise and attempt to communicate with family and friends until we are blue in the face, but if they are not ready to hear what you have to say, they will not listen, so just laugh it out. Let it go. It's about being quieter. Then, we had to lie down and witness ourselves with our third eye. I was so clear and purified as though I was truly prepared for change.

TEARS ARE THE MOST BEAUTIFUL EXPRESSION

The next meditation that I participated in on this retreat was the hour of crying. This was easy for me to tap into, as it was easy to channel both my own suffering and the suffering of the world. The cry was for the world, then my family and friends, and then after being exhausted, it was for me. It was freeing to be able to cry as loud as I wished. Tears are among the most beautiful expressions, as they express the inexpressible and deepest feelings.

I felt so lucky that I could still cry. While I and all the other participants were all in tears, toward the end of the meditation, the instructor said, "Now cry the tears of gratitude." As if on cue, the tears of gratitude began to stream out. I was so thankful for this opportunity to go deep within myself and connect with my inner feelings, to connect with who I really am.

Because of this experience, my new end goal was about living there in that place, attaining the true self, and staying there. My mind and soul suddenly woke up. It wasn't about staying in Buddhism. Instead, I needed to immerse myself into a religion that would be more sustainable for my life. This was a life-altering three-day retreat.

STILLING THE MONKEY MIND

In my exploration of Buddhism, I followed teachers that taught in ways that spoke to my inner being. I was fortunate to find individuals who led inspiring weekend learning retreats and pilgrimages. The main focus of these events was to "still the monkey mind," a Chinese proverb that resonated with me, where one meditates to detach from distraction and slow down the active mind and quiet down your thoughts. After experiencing this silence, I began to see all aspects of my life with absolute clarity. It was an intensely calming practice and I still use some of these meditations that I learned years ago. Also, at these retreats, I learned to be thankful to a power greater than myself, to be thankful not just on Thanksgiving, but every day.

My teachers also emphasized that you can't expect the spirituality to keep you on a "never-ending high." There are also lows, and those lows help you to appreciate the beauty of the highs.

A Buddhist goal is to find a way to maintain a state of peace, and not to become unglued by the peaks and valleys. My teachers taught me that I need to accept that everything that happens in my life, the good and the bad, happens for a reason. As persons in the world, we all need to observe and learn from these occurrences. This is how I will overcome challenges.

SEEKING INNER STRENGTH

While at these retreats, my fellow participants and I were given many mantras and calming phrases to chant. My daughter Natalie finds one of these chants especially funny.

Who I am, nobody knows.
Where I Dwell! Everything Glows.
Wake up! Rise up! Surrender your Woes.
Wake up! Rise up! Surrender your Woes.

Often, when Natalie and I are spending time together, to break the monotony, we take turns singing it in different tunes. This is a nice way to connect to a beautiful memory of a powerful awakening that was taking place in me many years ago and to share it in the present with one of the most important people in my life. When we get inspired, and when we reach the top of the mountain, we can't expect to relay the experience in words. We need to show through our behavior and action what we have learned through our various experiences.

DON'T SIT ON THE FENCE TOO LONG

These major events of religious experimentation, which spanned a period of over five years in my life, opened a whole new world for me that I was excited to learn more about.

Unlike the Himalayan monks who rarely leave their monastery, I found myself thriving in the real world while using my Buddhist principles. I gained a lot of clarity from the retreats and I brought the positive energy with me when I left the weekend retreats. Imbued with renewed spirituality, I also felt a responsibility to my family and community to partake in the annual Jewish Holy Days rituals like never before. I felt and experienced more meaning in the celebration of these Holy Days, now that I was able to connect to my spiritual side more.

It gave these days a whole new meaning. I got to see the opportunity to create joy and laughter on these days. I saw the power in being holy and sacred. It becomes an opportunity to make it into an event.

My last most memorable two-day meditation retreat affected me in a very lasting way. In the last few hours of an emotionally exhilarating weekend, there were over one hundred people sitting on the floor in a large square room. Our teacher opened the last session of the weekend by saying, "Over the years I have sparked the hearts and souls of many. Some of you will choose to go back to the roots of your father's or mother's religion. Please don't feel bad about it. I am proud to be the catalyst. However, you can't straddle between two spiritual systems, because 'if you sit on the fence too long, you get hemorrhoids.'"

I have used this powerful phrase untold times. I am certain that this last message, delivered at the end of the retreat, was directed toward me. Although it was bittersweet to hear, it made a lot of sense that I was starting to genuinely experience the religion I was born into and was beginning to feel comfort and connection toward it. I learned you cannot cross the river with your feet in two different row boats. Hence, I threw myself into Judaism.

Chapter 14
RETURNING TO MY ROOTS

THE NEVER-ENDING SEARCH FOR MEANING

Only through spiritual aspirations and growth can we have great joy from this world. And spiritual aspirations don't necessarily have to mean following any one deity. According to the Merriam-Webster dictionary, the definition of the word "spirit" is "the force within a person that is believed to give the body life, energy, and power." Doing good deeds in this world is the most important aspect of one's existence, no matter what belief system one follows.

Immediately after the birth of my first-born son, and two years later with the birth of my son, Benjamin, I felt incredible joy and elation that they were healthy and perfect. I was grateful for these true gifts of life. I also felt that I contributed to my family's lineage. I was in a state of shock realizing that I was a partner to this miracle.

With this great responsibility of becoming a father, I began to seek teachers to find the answers I needed to understand the deeper meaning of life and raising children. I was committed to immersing myself daily for one hour with various inspirational rabbis. One of my instructors, Rabbi Yitz Summers, introduced me to one of the many yeshivas (a Jewish school with a literal interpretation "to sit down with a learning partner") on Beverly Drive in Los Angeles.

The learning experience transported me to study halls of past generations. The large, open, well-lit rooms were filled at all times of the day with hundreds of young and older men wearing white shirts and black pants. All were involved in lively conversation. Like everyone else, my instructor sat across from me, reading, interpreting, and delving deeper than ever into various topics that would ultimately deepen my knowledge and connection with the concept of a higher power.

To calm my discomfort of learning this new environment, Rabbi Summers started with a Mishnah (a 2,600-year-old written collection of the Jewish oral traditions, also known as the "oral Torah"). Among the thousands of teachings, it states the following tenets that I use to guide my character: "A responsible person has to always keep in mind the following: Be quiet in the presence of the more educated./ Listen to your friend without interrupting./ Do not answer in haste, rather wait to fully consider the response."

I felt reassured from that first lesson that I was on the right track. After all, silence has been my friend for many years. It reaffirmed that it was okay not to know, and to be an observer taking in the world of ideas and insights of people wiser and more educated than myself.

I remember being excited to know that Judaism is the source of much religious thought, and that the concept of silence is the single most important quality in attaining wisdom.

I began collecting pearls of wisdom that applied to my life. I kept meticulous notes in case I need to reference the information about a topic. Now when I travel, I always take a batch of wisdom and carry it with me to stay focused so I stay on course.

One of the most influential instructors I still study with is Yigal Kutai. His mantra is that the ultimate pleasure is always being connected to God. The way a child feels holding his parent's hand—safe, secure, strong, and connected—is how we as adults can feel that same sense of serenity and security, by being connected to the higher power, like holding your hand as a child.

By connecting to the divine we separate our souls from our physical being. Yigal explains that we work hard our entire life, feeding, cleaning, exercising, and satisfying our outer shell. We need to do the same for our *neshama*—our soul and our innermost essential being needs the same care and attention as our outer shell. When we release the soul from the prison of the body, and when we notice and become aware of it, it gets easier to connect. We become connected to an immense treasure trove. How much money we have, the size of our home, or the car we drive becomes irrelevant.

The conditioning of the soul for a Jewish boy begins at the age of thirteen—the Bar Mitzvah. This is when a boy becomes a man and he is obligated to connect, to pray, three times a day. The prayers were written by eighty-eight wise men in 70 AD after the destruction of the second temple in Jerusalem and the Jews were exiled from their homeland again.

Unfortunately, I missed my Bar Mitzvah experience as my family and I had just arrived in Sydney when I was turning thirteen, and my parents were preoccupied with settling into new surroundings. This is why I take such pride in learning the *parasha* and continue to study and learn every week with a rabbi.

LASHON HARA: THE POTENCY OF NEGATIVITY

In all the texts, in particular the Torah (Old Testament), there is an emphasis repeatedly about the importance of avoiding gossip, negative speech, and judging people unfavorably, which is called Lashon Hara in Hebrew. Rabbi Summers references the teaching that states that we have two mouths with which we speak. One in which we pray, meditate, praise, and speak positively. And the second mouth from which we judge unfavorably and speak slanderously. It is inconceivable that with the same mouth we can do both.

I felt that this concept was pertinent to my life. Especially so with advent of social media, by which we are bombarded with gossip and the chain of negative stories, one after another. There are crimes committed, diseases, disasters, war zones, and all the terrible things that are happening around us in the world. The more chaos and hysteria in the story, the more coverage it always gets. Every news source has the same objective and that is to ensure that whoever is tuned in does not switch to another channel.

As a result of this lesson, I find myself constantly repeating we must have faith. Having faith is like putting down roots, so when the wind blows hard, we have the stability in our lives, because of these deep roots. Even though the world is still far from being perfect, the sun still comes up every day, without exception. We tend to look at the world like we look at the sheet of paper with the black spot. When asked what we see on the sheet, we declare, "It's a black spot," and we ignore the white paper. We only seem to emphasize the black spot. We should take time to reflect on the big picture, which is the white paper, and not get bogged down with the minutiae of the black spot.

Now that I am older, I have come to the realization that I cannot avoid negative energy in people. I am sensitive to the dark cloud that happens when I'm around certain individuals. I feel my mind begin to rattle, the feeling is destabilizing, thoughts begin to become hazy and I stop thinking straight. When I see or sense this dark cloud of negative energy coming, I have learned to respectfully remove myself from the situation. I take a long deep breath and look for the exit door while saying my goodbyes to everyone. I rationalize that it's not my problem. It's their negativity that they impose on others. I don't fall for this guilt trip anymore. I draw boundaries and remind myself that it's not my problem.

ALL OF WISDOM IN ONE WORD

In thinking about wisdom, a story comes to mind involving Yigal Kutai. The incident happened after he gave a long and deep lecture to a serious and learned audience. An elderly woman stood up and asked him if he could summarize all wisdom into one word. The question surprised the audience. Yigal began stroking his beard while looking at the woman, obviously thinking deeply about her question. After a minute of silence, he turned to the woman and said, "Discipline. In one word: all of life is about discipline."

I began keeping the kosher laws twenty years ago. The main reason I observed these laws was to discipline myself to follow a system, even if I did not understand the laws. Even though all laws relating to keeping kosher are devoid of rational explanation, I still chose this path. I realized that this is not an easy request of me because I love to be in control. However, by relinquishing control, I needed to feel genuinely humble enough to accept the rules and become servant to the Divine, even though there is no explanation as to why.

Despite all the learning, I resisted keeping the important ritual of kashrut: abiding by the Jewish laws of foods that are allowed to be consumed and the foods that are forbidden for Jewish people to eat. The impetus to observe the dietary laws began on my fourth wedding anniversary. Karla and I made a reservation at one of LA's best restaurants. We both ordered an endive and hearts of palm, as an appetizer. Karla's salad had an additional component that we did not expect. Half-inch green and white worms began raising their heads from behind and in between the lettuce. Shocked, alarmed, and bewildered, we called the waiter and advised him of our discovery. I told Karla this had to be a message from God. Worms in our salad? It meant that it was time to start keeping kosher.

Kosher laws require a rabbi stationed in the kitchen to supervise every aspect of the food production process. This is a reason kosher food is more expensive. I made a commitment that night that I was going to only eat in restaurants that follow my dietary restrictions. I am still doing it to this day.

THE COMFORT OF RITUALS

"Ritual" is a large component of all religions. Rituals are the foundation to all traditions. The power of repeating rituals and traditions bring comfort and a sense of some sort of predictability in a world that changes every second of which you have no control.

My favorite ritual is the daily workout I inculcated into my psyche since I was twenty-one years old, and just arrived in LA. Skipping my daily workout is not an option. I am dedicated, and every day I strengthen my outer shell. In my early days, I was regular in my attendance at the gym, then running, and then yoga. Now, I continue a workout regimen that includes swimming. I do it every day, whether I am tired or not. Thank you to Carrie Ceryes for teaching my entire family to swim for the past twenty-five years.

"Shabbat is the day in which God ended his work which he had done. And God blessed the seventh day and sanctified it, because in it he rested from all the work which he created and performed."

Shabbat, which is also the day of rest, is another subject I love learning about. I've mentioned the power of Shabbat as I was growing up in Israel and Australia. It's central to the Torah and has become an integral part of my life. The Shabbat experience is so significant to our *neshama* that it occurs every week. It gives us the opportunity to pause, reflect, and recharge. Interestingly whenever the Torah mentions

Shabbat, it first mentions "six days of work." It's a celebration of the work which is completed for those six days. The week ends and begins with Shabbat.

This had immense relevance to my life as I was driven to achieve objectives and goals every single day, week after week. The rule at my home from sundown on Friday night until sunset on Saturday night for everyone, including the children, was essentially to "power down." We control time; it does not control us. We prep and shower to get dressed in crisp clean clothes. It was the time to turn off all electronics for twenty-four hours. We do not conduct any business, allowing us twenty-four hours of no economic concerns, no buying or selling of any product. I stop thinking about the price of things and instead focus on the value of things.

On Shabbat, Jewish people can't sell or buy things. We can't work or pay others to work for us. We are not to "create" anything including putting on electricity, watching, or using any electronics, cutting, drawing, cooking, or cleaning. Our only goal is to spend quality time with our family and friends and not be distracted by anything else. One day of the whole week, we dedicate ourselves to nourishing our families with our attention and our time. It's an opportunity to stop and observe the results of my week's work and I get to relax and enjoy family and friends.

From the holy, to the ordinary, to the holy again. We are instructed to prepare for Shabbat as if we are leaving for a twenty-four-hour voyage. After sunset Friday evening, we cannot prepare any longer. Creative activity, in the physical sense at least, is frozen. What was prepared may be enjoyed and what was not is forever lost. Shabbat is the dimension of being, not becoming.

I plan for Shabbat properly to ensure that friends and family are invited for Friday night and Saturday lunch, as we create menus for the weekly celebrations. Friday morning, I go to my favorite bakery and buy two or three different types of challah bread and stock up on a selection of quality kosher wines and plan the menu for the week-end. I also print out and brush up on the week's reading of the Torah so that I can lead the conversation at the Shabbat table and discuss the weekly portion to be read at the synagogue on Saturday morning and analyze its relevance to our lives today.

Rabbi Jonathan Sachs, London's chief rabbi, who has regularly visited LA, often said in reference to Shabbat, "Without the ability to be inactive at least once a week, all of our subsequent activity has no meaning." We need inactivity at least once a week. The task of powering down is filled with activity, but it is an activity we are not accustomed to during the week.

During the week, we work, we build, and we create. On Shabbat, we cease to continue the process of creation and stop to "smell the roses" without guilt, just enjoying the ultimate joy of that which was created. Anyone and everyone should give this notion a try. It's healthy for the spirit no matter what you believe in.

Over the years, I have invited numerous friends from different faiths to Friday night Shabbat dinner or Saturday lunch. Several of these friends, some Christian and Hindu, were so moved by the experience of turning off their daily distractions and tasks that they decided to observe, as best they could or in their own way, this ritual with their family and friends.

My favorite part to this day is the singing and humming of timeless melodies that hold both nostalgia and tradition for this weekly special ritual. The Shabbat message told for generations is: "Waste no time, build constantly, direct all activities during the week toward correct goals."

As the sun sets Saturday evening and three stars become visible, we perform a five-minute ceremony called Havdalah (meaning "distinguishing the holy from the mundane"). We light an intertwined candle that has three wicks, smell spices, and drink a cup of wine—all performed because there's a feeling of letdown that holiness has left, so by performing the ritual of Havdalah, we revive our soul in preparation for the beginning of a new week.

From birth we are obligated to teach our children the ritual of reciting Modeh Ani, which we recite daily upon waking, while still in bed, before our feet touch the ground. This prayer thanks God for renewing every person as new creation on a daily basis and we express our gratitude to God for restoring our soul each morning.

The other prayer is called Shema, which is the centerpiece of the daily morning and evening services and is considered the most essential prayer in all of Judaism. It is affirmation of God's singularity and kingship. The prayer essentially says that you shall love God with all your heart, with all your soul, and with all your might. Impress these rules upon your children, recite them when you stay at home and when you are away, when you lie down and when you get up. Bind them as a sign in your hand and let them serve as a symbol on your forehead, inscribe them on your doorposts of your house and your gates. This basically explains a particular way the faith should be lived—love God with all your being and teach your children to recite this prayer when they wake up and lie down to go to sleep for the night.

DEATH: AN INTRINSIC PART OF LIFE

Upon my mother's passing, I experienced a whole new part of being an adult, one that I knew very little about. My siblings and I flew her body to Jerusalem to be buried in the same cemetery where her parents are laid to rest. After the burial, my family chose my home in Jerusalem to be the place where we would sit Shiva, where the mourning family eats, prays, and sleeps together for seven days while friends and family come visit and pay tribute.

Sitting Shiva is very intense mourning ritual that allows you to grieve properly for your loss as a family. During Shiva, the family sits on low chairs all day long, and is not supposed to change clothes from the day of the burial while having a tear in their shirts to symbolize grief and loss. I had our LA Rabbi, Moshe Benzaquen, join us in Israel to assist us with all the formalities. The rabbi was with us most of the days into the evening, explaining the rules relating to mourning.

After two days, it seemed as though weeks had passed. We were living, learning, thinking, and focusing every waking moment on reflecting about my mom's life and legacy. We were telling stories about her and hearing about her from her closest childhood friends. Many of the visitors were my mom's nephews and nieces who visited long into the night for at least six full days. It was a comforting process, since sitting Shiva allows one to mourn by not having any distractions from feeling the pain of grief, especially while a family is all together to give each other the love and support needed to get through this difficult time.

Before Mom's death, going to funerals and making condolence visits was extremely difficult for me. I was often thinking, What can I possibly say to help this person who just suffered a loss? It is awkward because there isn't anything that can really comfort a loss of a parent or a child.

I feel that I had always been lacking knowledge in how to console a mourner. I recall very clearly that it did not matter what people said to me or my family—it just wouldn't help relieve the pain. But when a person came to visit, and as they walked into the room with a sad look on their face about my loss, it was immediately comforting. I felt cared about. It was the same with friends calling from other countries with condolences. Just hearing the tone of sadness in their voice, I felt enormous comfort, love, and support.

Now I go to these visits with a lighter heart, planning not to say much at all. It does not matter that I cannot possibly know what pain the mourner is going through, or how well I know the deceased. There is no need to worry about that. What really matters is just to be there and show that you care for that person's loss.

It wasn't until my mom's passing that I learned that a son mourning a parent's death had to recite the Mourners' Kaddish prayer three times a day for twelve months after that death. The reason for this special prayer is that Jewish tradition teaches that following death, our physical body decays but our soul returns to its source—to the Divine. By uttering this two-minute Aramaic prayer, I was exalting the power of life in honor of my mom. Saying Kaddish is a very serious commitment. It confirmed that I entered adulthood, that I'd matured. As long as Mom was alive, I felt that I was still a child in some way. Now I honor her memory. My mom was always kind, giving great parenting advice and always supportive of me. I realize so much of my soul comes from her. I recognize and never forget her special and unique character.

The first seven days I did this ritual with my father, brothers, and family members at the house. Upon returning to LA, it was not as easy for the remainder of the twelve months. I would begin the day by attending synagogue at sunrise. I would end the day by going back to synagogue just before sunset and saying the Kaddish to honor my mom two more times. The Kaddish kept me connected to her. After the twelve months of reciting the Kaddish, I missed not being able to say it daily. I was sanctifying God's name in her name to honor her.

Another stringent rule that I respected was not to actively listen to music or attend parties, festive events, and celebrations for twelve months. This was difficult because I love to have ongoing background classical and jazz music for a sense of tranquility. I also did not attend any celebrations, weddings, and other social gatherings. These restrictions can be difficult, sometimes seeming impossible, especially for one who has an active life with professional and personal obligations. This period definitely required a strong showing of discipline. On the annual anniversary of her passing in January 2009, my siblings and I are obligated to recite the Kaddish prayer. We sponsor a festive meal for the family and community in memory of the deceased parent—in this case, our beloved mother.

While you may never sit Shiva, recite the Kaddish, or read a page of the Torah, you can still make your own ritual filled with love and discipline.

MEANING OF THE MOMENT

I belong to a CEO board which is a tight-knit, select group of highly accomplished and experienced CEOs/business owners/entrepreneurs who work together to become the best we can be for our companies. Our chairperson, Shel Brucker, who has been a great friend and mentor, leads all our meetings and helps guide us. He delves into our personal and professional lives to see the areas that we can improve individually for the betterment of our families, friends, and businesses and to be inspiring leaders who lead outstanding organizations to create extraordinary impact. Three times a year, Shel invites guest speakers to inspire and motivate us in various aspects of our lives.

One of these speakers from New York, Brett Pyle, whose focus was the power of communication, talked about a book I had previously read, *Man's Search for Meaning* by Viktor E. Frankl, which my brother David introduced me to as a teenager, that greatly impacted my life.

Frankl was a Holocaust survivor and a psychologist. In 1939 he was rounded up by the Nazis from his home in Austria and transported on a cattle train to four different concentration camps, including Auschwitz. While he was in the concentration camp, when it appeared that no one would survive, he questioned whether under these circumstances, life was ultimately void of any meaning.

The answer came to Frankl when he had to surrender his clothing and was given the rags of an inmate who had been sent to the gas chamber on arrival at the camp. In the pocket of the clothes, he found a page torn out of a Jewish prayer-book. The *Shema Yisrael*, a daily prayer that he remembered his father saying every day when he was a boy, was written on this torn piece of paper. When he found it, he felt the prayer was his reminder to challenge himself to live the life that he had written and to practice what he preached. For the next two and half years he suffered starvation and humiliation in four concentration camps that he was transferred to.

Being a psychologist, he decided to use the time he was in torturous labor camps to study "who will die and who will live." He was given the opportunity to help new prisoners get over the shock and fear of coming to the concentration camps. He realized that those who learned that they lost their loved ones felt like they had no hope and had nothing to live for. They did not care anymore. Those like himself, who had loved ones still alive, had hope with a strength and power to live. Frankl, during his speaking engagements, explained, despite the title of his book, we all have to find the meaning in every moment of our lives. It is a never-ending process because there are different meanings to our lives during different times in our lives. Many search for meaning but will not have a definitive answer. It is what we do in the moment that creates the meaning.

The lesson Frankl learned was that no matter what your circumstance is, do all that you can to find meaning in it. If it is not evident immediately, search until you find that meaning because the search for meaning in one's life is a never-ending process. We are all searching for meaning at every moment in our lives.

THE POWER OF THE WORD

During his lecture, Brett Pyle asked listeners, "Does anyone know the blessing for water in Judaism?"

I proudly raised my hand and asked him in what language did he want to hear it in—Hebrew or English? He answered, "Say it in Hebrew" and I did. He then interpreted what I said into English for everyone to understand. "Blessed you God, Master of the Universe that everything was created by your word," he said.

Pyle continued, "Gentlemen, ladies, it's about 'the Word.' It's about the power of the Word and what we can do with that power."

He went on to say, "I was impacted by the power of words as a child. I was eleven years old, my dad had me weed the grass, and I did. I weeded it for a couple of hours, because I wanted my dad happy. And I did it, and I did it, and I did it, and I was sweating, and I did everything that I could do to do it well and up to my dad's standards. Finally, my dad comes out there, and he says to me, 'Brett, I see a weed. And another over here.' And, I will never forget that because what it told me was that I would never be good enough. Recently, my eleven-year-old son said to me, 'Hey Dad, how did I do washing your car?' Since the car he had just washed still had soap marks on it, I walked him back to the car and pointed out that he had not done the task of washing off the soap suds or drying the car correctly, and I told him so. I instantly found myself having fallen into my dad's trap of telling my son that what he had done will also never be good enough. With my disapproval, and noticing my son's reaction to me, I realized that I was doing the same thing my dad had done to me when I was eleven years old. Fifteen minutes later, I went to my son's room and apologized profusely. I told him that I made the same mistake that my dad had made with me and that I would be more aware of the words I would use in the future."

Brett Pyle's words spoke directly to me. The power of the word "apology" is so important. The message that he delivered to us that day profoundly struck me. I understood the power and effect your word can have, long term, if you don't use the right words. Looking at the bigger picture, it makes me wonder why we wait until our lives are almost over to make amends, apologize, or forgive our loved ones. Why would anyone want to hold onto resentment and bad feelings toward others until their very last moment in life to jeopardize their legacy and what they leave behind in the hearts of loved ones. It is important to reach out and tell those that you care about that you love them, forgive them, and apologize to them.

THE KIND ACT OF CIVILITY

Civility, a book by Stephen L. Carter, tells a story of a young black boy who moves into a predominantly white Washington, DC, neighborhood in 1966, and the sadness of the surrounding environment. During the first week he lived there, he would sit with his siblings on the front porch. People passed by his house all day and no one made the time to stop by to say "hello" and welcome them to the neighborhood. But one time, a Jewish woman across the street screamed out, "Hey there, children, I've got a plate of sandwiches here I made just for you. I will be right with you."

He wrote what he was thinking at that moment, "This is so ugly here, I hate this city. I wish we didn't come here." Then suddenly, Sara, the neighbor across the street, is there at his house with a plate full of sandwiches. This little act became a life-changing moment.

Carter, now a Yale law professor, social critic, and scholar, lectures and he claims, "I still remember the taste of those sandwiches—those peanut butter and jelly sandwiches—made by that woman who changed my whole attitude toward people, and toward the world."

Steve Carter teaches that the lack of "civility" and society's loss of basic good manners have become a casualty of our postmodern culture. He defines civility as "the sum of the many sacrifices we are called upon to make for the sake of living together." For everyone to get along, we need to embrace the basics of regularly placing the common good above one's own immediate self-interest and to hold back impulsive reactions to satisfy selfish purposes. He reinforces this ideology with everyday examples, such as exercising self-restraint to not cut off another driver in traffic or not yell at the TV screen when someone is expressing a different point of view.

I love that story. Stories like that inspire me. I have collected so many stories like that to share with others. While we are busy dealing with our own lives, we must remember to also take the time to inspire others and show small acts of civility that will have profound effects on others and their outlook on the world.

IT ONLY WORKS WHEN YOU SHOW UP

Life is meant to be engaging, and in order to succeed, you cannot wait for things to come to you. You have to get actively involved. Chances are, positive opportunities will not come knocking at your door seeking you out. You have to actively participate, or as I have said many times, you have to show up to be part of the game. When you do, you will be surprised at the results that follow. It has happened to me, and it can happen to you, too.

With my family, I want to be compassionate, helpful, and loving toward them. With my children, I want to give them guidance by setting a good example for them, and to encourage them to make the best decisions they can in their own lives. In business, I want to have the members of my team take pride in and responsibility for what they do, and to show our guests and customers a positive experience in every way.

I love the fact that I have surrounded myself with the closeness of good people and have come to know what is good and what is healthy for me. I feel very happy and fulfilled in my life right now. Hospitality is, has been, and continues to be the driving force in my life. My Zen guru once told me, "If they tell you something is an original, it's a lie.

Everything is a derivative." That gave me the stamp of approval to emulate successful ideas I've seen or read about from others.

To be gracious and kind toward people is not a goal; it is a lifestyle. As I have mentioned, I want the people who come to stay at our hotels to expect the best experience, and to come away with the feeling that my team and I have exceeded their expectations in every way.

THIS TOO SHALL PASS

I close this chapter using King Solomon's search for the perfect message to inscribe onto his ring. The goal was always to be reminded to live a life not too sad and not too euphoric for the good days and the bad: "This too shall pass."

I feel that the greatest accomplishment is to be able to help other people find their way to a better life, and to a more fulfilling life. No matter what you believe in your day-to-day spiritual journey, you can always count on the mere fact that any negative or despairing experience won't last forever. Whenever you are down, tell yourself that this too shall pass.

Chapter 15
TEACHERS ARE THE HEROES

TEACHERS CHANGE LIVES

According to Greek writer Nikos Kazantzakis, "True teachers use themselves as bridges over which they invite their students to cross. Then having facilitated their crossing, joyfully collapse, encouraging them to create bridges of their own."

I have always admired teachers, and my dad is a large part of my inspiration for my involvement in education. Being a teacher, Dad always made my siblings and me feel that teachers are every society's unsung heroes, and we should go out of our way to honor and remember them.

When a desire to teach grows in a person, you can't stop it. It becomes an unstoppable need to impact people's lives. Teachers that make an impact are those that are extremely dedicated and passionate about their profession. According to Joseph Campbell, "A hero is someone who has given his or her life to something bigger than oneself." Some of the greatest teachers in the history of the world, including Buddha, Mahavira, Jesus, Moses, and Mohammed, all spent their entire lives teaching.

Unfortunately, teaching seems to be a slowly declining profession, which is not good for our society. Those of us with the means should look to protect and grow the teaching profession.

After all, it is the teacher who prepares our children to succeed in the world. They need a strong collaboration with the parents and must actively seek to engage the parents' attention to assist in the home.

I hope that talented, smart young people will not be deterred from entering the field of education due to current social and economic challenges. Education should be a highly desired career path. Concepts and technology are constantly being developed. That hopefully will unburden teachers of grunt-work and leave them more time to stress the mentoring and student development of young people. Teachers should be made to feel that there is hope. They can go beyond their role as teachers and become mentors to kids.

EDUCATION IS KEY

The first thing that Moses announced when he brought the Jews out of Egypt was their new mission. He told them, "You must educate your children. You must not let them forget where you came from. Tell them our story. For us to become a truly free people, we have got to educate our children. If we don't educate our children, we don't have a civilization."

That is why the Jewish population—despite all its hardships over the years—continues to thrive. I believe that the viewed importance of education in the Jewish religion was so inbred and given such importance, that we as a people are compelled to make that impact on the world.

I feel that I have a responsibility, wherever possible, to provide a platform where teachers are empowered to communicate with each one of their students. Every student possesses the capacity to influence countless numbers of hearts and minds. Teachers have the ability to change lives and to nurture students who will, hopefully, make the world a better place for all of us.

As capable adults, we have a responsibility to foster the life skills of our youth in every society. I feel I have a personal responsibility to assist in preparing the children in our communities to go into the world engaging and making it a better place. For me, it's gratifying to impact a child's life, to develop and encourage their skills. Our youth are our hope for change in the world. They are our most precious natural resource.

When we bolster the skills and talents of young people, we are not only helping them—we are receiving a benefit as well. It is gratifying to impact a person's life, to help them develop and sharpen their skills. We all need to be constantly inspired and mentally stimulated.

THE SMALLEST GASH IN A YOUNG SAPLING RESULTS IN A DEFORMITY OF THE TREE

If a knife happens to cut a gash in a grown tree, it would make very little consequence to the further growth of the tree. However, if you were to cut a gash in a young sapling, that same scar would grow in size and intensity, along with the tree.

The same point can be made about educators and their students. Positive or negative reinforcement in a child's life can impact the adult that child becomes. Being a teacher is not easy. Luckily, despite the low financial return, the majority of teachers are dedicated and passionate about their profession. For them, it just doesn't have to be about their paycheck, although that too needs to be a bigger part of their reward.

Being a teacher has to be wired into a person's DNA. When a desire to teach grows in a person, it cannot be stopped. I know, first-hand, how important it is to give kids the support, love, and nurturing they need in their youth, and I want to do whatever I can do to assist in offering the best education for as many children as possible. During my own experience with education, I felt the teachers were not in tune with the children, not giving them enough attention. The system failed me in that way. In today's social and political climate, more than ever before, teachers must know the psychology of working with the kids.

As a result of my own childhood experiences, I feel strongly that I must encourage and support that parent-teacher partnership effort. I want to recognize and honor educators that bring new innovations to the profession.

In my community in Los Angeles, there are several families that have devoted significant resources and funds to ensure that promote quality education. Mitch Julis, in honor of his parents Maurice and Thelma Julis, who were both educators, funds a creative program that inspires and mentors teachers and faculty members to become more successful as teaching professionals.

Lowell and Michael Milken, through their Milken Family Foundation, have an annual event honoring teachers in schools in forty-eight states across the United States. They hold their event in Los Angeles at the Luxe Hotel on Sunset. They honor individual teachers in the school system who have shown great progress and innovation in inspiring their students and go above and beyond to help and mentor their students. The Milken Award is not just to honor the individual teachers receiving them—it honors education as whole and the foundation awards each outstanding teacher with a $15,000 check.

Marty Cooper is one of those people who is not only driven to success in his profession, but also has a deep desire to contribute to the betterment of the community. His firm, Cooper Communications, Inc., has represented a broad range of clients. Previously, Cooper was senior vice president of marketing and communications for Playboy Enterprises, Inc. where he created the Playboy Jazz Festival at The Hollywood Bowl. He is the only person to have reported to both Walt Disney and Hugh Hefner.

Marty feels today's youth need the guidance and support necessary to achieve a better life for themselves and the impetus to contribute to the society at large. He has spent more than a decade as a member of the board of The Boys & Girls Club. Their mission is to inspire and enable all young people, especially those from disadvantaged circumstances, to realize their full potential as productive, responsible, and caring citizens.

Over the years, Barbara Shore has offered love and guidance to several youth who had been removed from unsafe family situations and placed in institutions for at-risk children. According to Barbara, "It is so important to help a child who doesn't have the resources to help themselves. They may need a role model, financial assistance, or they simply may need encouragement. Without guidance, they may not be able to reach their potential. It doesn't take a lot of energy, but what a difference it makes to them when they hear their dreams are truly attainable and know you believe in them."

Peter Samuelson, an educator, media executive, film producer, and founder of First Star, is another one of those special people. First Star pioneers support programs to launch foster children into productive lives and careers through higher education. The statistics are devastating, with less than 3 percent of foster youth earning a bachelor's degree and over 50 percent of them becoming homeless, staying on welfare, or becoming incarcerated. First Star creates pathways to college for foster youth by reinforcing the importance of a higher education.

I met several eighteen-year-old foster kids at a fundraiser for the program. I asked the kids if everything I had heard about First Star was true. They explained that living in their circumstance was very difficult with no parents around, let alone any idea of what the college experience is like or what it can offer for their future. They said that Peter Samuelson, whom they call "Grandpa," arranges for groups of twenty kids at a time to attend one of fourteen participating campuses, including UCLA, around the country. There, they are accommodated for four weeks over the summer and are given housing, meals, and the ability to take lectures of their choice with top university professors. This opportunity gives them an insight of what they can work toward and the ability to make their academic dreams come true. Ninety-nine percent of First Star youth graduate high school and 90 percent of them go on to higher education. This, to me, is a true testament to what heroes we have among us in our communities.

These types of organizations truly inspire the great minds of tomorrow, no matter what the environment and circumstances they come from.

It's the small seeds that we nurture that will eventually grow to impact the world and make a better society.

THE HARKHAM FAMILY COMMITMENT TO EDUCATION

In 1982, I had the privilege of traveling to Israel and meeting the Prime Minister Menachem Begin. To this day I consider Begin to be a giant in the history of the creation of the state of Israel. He was wearing a fresh dark business suit and red tie, and large black-rimmed glasses. My objective was to propose to the prime minister a PR campaign at a time when Israel was receiving horribly negative exposure worldwide. Burson-Marsteller/Young & Rubicam, one of the top public relations companies in the US that I was working with at the time, had offered assistance to help Israel with their global image. They offered to launch this campaign for a flat fee.

I told Prime Minister Begin about this during my visit with him, and I hoped he would accept their help. He gratefully acknowledged my thoughtfulness. Putting his hand on my hand, as we sat in his very humble office, he said, "PR is not going to save us. Two things will: one is AIPAC, the American Israel Political Action Committee that educates US senators and congressmen of the Israel-Arab conflict, and the other equally important—if not more important thing—is to make sure our Jewish community outside of Israel must not lose their connection with Israel. We must continue to teach traditional Jewish values, love of Israel, and Jewish history." He also expressed concern that this global educational network must be affordable to preserve that connection.

His words had a profound impact on me and they have inspired—and continue to inspire—my actions through the years. This is what started my interest and commitment to honor and strong Jewish education in my community.

My family and I are privileged to have been involved in the building of several schools to accomplish this goal. One of them, The Harkham Hillel Academy in Beverly Hills on Olympic Boulevard and Doheny Drive, presently has over 500 students enrolled in it. It is now honored as a blue-ribbon accredited school and it is successfully thriving. The current principal, Baruch Sufferin, has been honored on behalf of the school, with the President's Award of Excellence for Education. This makes me very proud.

HARKHAM-GAON ACADEMY

In 2013, my rabbi, friend, and mentor, Rabbi Moises Benzaquen, had a dream to build a more affordable high school in the Los Angeles area. He had already started an educationally focused program that attracted fifty kids, which ultimately became difficult to sustain economically. It needed a complete triage effort, and so together we renamed it GAON Academy.

Harkham-GAON Academy is a fully accredited modern Jewish high school located at JCC that serves the greater Los Angeles area. The center provides a terrific location, featuring classrooms, three basketball courts, an Olympic-size swimming pool, and a variety of community space.

We have a diverse population of students from differing socioeconomic backgrounds, academic levels, and levels of observance. HGA students access their secular curriculum through online educational programming at school while our teachers are there in the classrooms to assist and guide them, offering a modernized, blended, and personalized experience and mentoring. However, this school is different from a regular high school in many ways. Harkham-GAON Academy provides an affordable educational option that spotlights Jewish heritage for those kids whose families desire a private education. Yet, this school strives to give those kids a superior education that will prepare them to get into great colleges and will give them the power and the skill to be aware of their Jewish values and roots at the same time.

The students learn at their own pace, using the best online teaching programs for all the critical secular subjects. All the books, learning materials, tests, and assessments are digital and interactive. The teachers are at the back of the class and provide one-on-one tutoring and mentoring for those students that have questions, fall behind, or need extra attention.

My goal is to make this a successful model for education, with the hope of creating similar GAON pods in other JCCs in cities around the country.

SHAKESPEARE ASKED, "WHAT'S IN A NAME?"

It was the kids who actually came up with the name "GAON" in reference to the school. The school is named in memory of three Jewish teenagers that were kidnapped and killed in Israel in 2014. "GAON" also means "genius" in Hebrew, so the name serves two purposes. It is sometimes forgotten that the death of these three boys likely saved the entire state of Israel. If not for the extensive search for the boys, the terrorist group Hamas would have—at a time of its choosing—streamed thousands of guerilla fighters through these same tunnels they had created to capture towns and military outposts. It was during the search for these three missing students that Israeli soldiers found these tunnels, some of which were dug all the way to Jerusalem. Hamas fighters stored Israeli army uniforms in the tunnels to be used as a guise for their plan to kill and capture while the Israeli army would have no time to organize.

The kidnapping of the three boys—Gilad, Ayal, and Naftali—united the nation that led to an offensive military operation that lasted eight days, the return of prisoners to jail, and to the entire country agreeing to launch a ground invasion. We are honored that the parents of these three boys accepted this tribute and concept in memory of their sons. Their deaths ultimately saved so many lives.

TEACHERS ARE THE HEROES OF OUR COMMUNITY

I am proud to have been associated with great educators who gave so much to their students. They do not receive enough gratitude from the students, parents, and the entire community. Our teachers are every society's unsung heroes.

In a person's transition from one level of education to another, they need increasingly stronger core values to live by, in order to deal with the new and different environment they find themselves in.

Moving from elementary school, to middle school, to high school, to college, and finally, to real life in a fast and competitive world is a difficult, competitive, and traumatic process. Preparing the kids to venture into the world, and to become independent of their parents, is our fundamental goal as educators.

Education should not be uniform. One size does not fit all in this case, unlike in law and order, which must be the same for everyone. I learned firsthand that when we are being educated, sometimes a person requires more time, more effort, and more concern than another. Education must be tailor-made.

You can't just send children to school and hope for the best. Parents should get involved in children's lives. Furthermore, because children spend so much of their time in school, every adult who comes into contact with a child has a direct bearing on shaping their future.

Over the years, my hotels have hosted educator-recognition events. These programs recognize the unsung heroes that nurture our kids every day. In addition to teacher recognition, we have provided fresh paint, playgrounds, and cookie bakes at the hotel for the young kids from local schools. We have also hosted various department tours for the older kids, thereby acquainting them with a variety of career options in hospitality. We've donated benches, water fountains, and grass playing fields, all geared to improving the students' educational environment to help elevate the learning experience. Just as teaching is a lifelong commitment, learning is a lifelong process. I'm committed to doing what I can to ensure that children have access to quality education. There are many organizations working toward this end that need our support, but there is always room for one more. We can all make a difference.

BRINGING EDUCATION TO FORGOTTEN PLACES

Kindness cannot be only for the inner circle. We must go beyond. Several years ago, my nephew, Richie, realizing my love for education, invited me to partner with him in an organization he founded in

Sydney, Australia. We created Hark Angel Foundation, a registered Australian charity with the initiative to build one hundred schools that support children in obtaining an education. The end goal of this is to break the cycle of poverty. The reason I was so attracted to this organization is that they have people on the ground ensuring that the money received reaches the right sources.

In selecting sites for the schools, we seek out areas with no learnfacilities at all. Existing "schools" are usually overcrowded in dilapidated structures where kids are educated in outdoor settings in unbearable heat. The common thread in all these places is that the older generation desperately wants their kids to receive an education in order to rise in the world but did not have the means to provide it. In our preliminary research, we found that in Third-World countries, over 80 percent of the students over the age of twelve do not receive any additional education. As a result, they are destined for low-paying jobs or no jobs at all. The children now understand the only way to beat poverty is to get an education, and then to hopefully come back and assist their community.

The first school was built in 2012 in Kenya for the Masai people. Richie traveled there, spent time with the community, and made a documentary while there, which focused on their need for education.

The other six schools were built between 2015 and 2019 in Myanmar, one of the most impoverished countries in the world. Our organization founded schools in a large farming community there that had been suffering for several years from a bad drought. Today, these schools we built serve over 1,600 kids and are expanding.

I just returned from an incredible journey to Myanmar (Burma) with my nephew, Richie, to visit our newest school in Burma, in a remote village. The communities and people were so welcoming and happy though they experienced many hardships with their lack of food and living circumstances. They face their challenges with true grace and dignity. They welcomed us as guests, opened the doors of their huts, and offered us food and drink, though they do not have a lot. As I handed out notebooks to the students in the classroom, their enthusiasm was contagious. They clearly realized that through education, they could impact the future of their villages. The beauty and richness of the people was overwhelming, and the entire trip was a life-altering experience.

The village held a ceremony to celebrate the school opening. The village Community Council now owns the school and they will provide the teachers and maintenance for all six primary schools. In addition, the Community Council pledged At the recep a woman was hosting foreign volunteers when Richie happened to meet her nephew, Philip. We were honored to be their guests for the celebration.

It is imperative to give every child the best education possible. This gives them the confidence to put these ideas and teachings into effect in their communities and all over the world. The word "impossible" should be removed from their vocabulary.

INSPIRING MINDS

My nephew Richie introduced me to an incredible story. While he was traveling to Kenya, he was hosted by a family. At the reception, a woman was hosting volunteers when Richie happened to meet her nephew Philip.

Philip lives in southern Kenya and comes from very humble beginnings and he inspired Richie to help him with his education. Philip lost both of his parents when he was very young, and his older brother raised him. They struggled but his brother sent Philip to school every day, nonetheless. He went back to his aunt's house for high school so he could work for her to make some money.

Richie helped him with funds to finish his studies in high school. Philip was a very good student and was called by a university in Nairobi to study community development and social work. After school he hopes to look for a job with an organization that focuses on the development of the communities. He wants to have an opportunity to educate and help eradicate poverty in his community, while giving hope to others like himself.

After hearing this, I committed to take care of Philip's full tuition for his university studies because we believe that he will come back and help his community. Philip is an absolute inspiration and we look forward to seeing what he will be able to accomplish.

AN ENLIGHTENING SOJOURN

At this point in my life, I realize that I have truly found my calling. Hospitality fuels my creativity, my welcoming nature, and my passion. Part of this passion is to share new places and new insights with my friends. To me that is real hospitality.

Ten years ago, I started an annual trip to my birthplace, Israel. On each trip I usually invite four or five friends and host them on a weeklong trip. I want them to have a chance to see and experience this country in a way that it should be seen, a country full of life, innovation, and spirituality, no matter what your background and religion happens to be.

Upon landing in Israel, guests are greeted at the gangway with a welcome sign from a VIP airport service representative, who whisks and escorts the passengers to a fast-track exclusive priority lane through security checks and passport control, then along to baggage claim.

We embark on our journey to my home in Jerusalem and tour the country for the next week. We have tour guides to take us to the Jewish, Muslim, and Christian quarters, visit historical sites like King David's Tomb, the Western Wall, Cardo tunnels, underground

Jerusalem excavations, the Temple Mount from a rooftop, Machaneh Yehuda Market: a culinary tasting tour of the Shuk. We go to Yad Vashem with a teacher / historian / lecturer, Ken Spiro, who gives a three-hour tour and a dose of reality at the museum. This museum in Jerusalem honors those who perished, and it also honors the righteous gentiles who hid and saved Jews from the Nazis.

Also, we travel to the lowest point on the earth, the Dead Sea, also known as the "sea of salt," which is more than fifteen million years old and contains ten times more salt than the ocean. While luxuriating there, we float in the sea on our backs without exerting any energy or pressure, and we are in blissful silence while surrounded by the desert. After spending time at the Dead Sea, my guests and I proceed to hear the story of the 1963 excavation of the stone fortress of Masada, which played a major role for Israel in forging its national identity. The final chapter of the Jewish Roman war from 73 to 74 CE took place there. We take a tram to the hilltop to hear the story of the 960 people who escaped from Jerusalem from the Romans. They took refuge in Masada for almost three years when the Romans came and breached the fortress. When the Romans entered, all 960 people preferred to die at their own hands rather than be enslaved or executed. They set fire to all the buildings and committed a mass suicide by drawing lots killing each other, since suicide is against Jewish belief, and left the one standing man to actually kill himself. This act marked the end of the Jewish-Roman war.

Next stop is a tour on the Mediterranean coast, Jaffa. It's an ancient port city and is famous for its association with biblical stories. The charming old city, with its narrow cobblestone streets and its beautiful broad view on the coastline, has been used as a port for thousands of years.

Then we visit Tel Aviv, Israel's most modern metropolis, also known as "the white city," because of the four thousand white buildings built in a unique fashion by Jewish architects in the Bauhaus manner. Our first stop every time is meeting with the principal of a successful start-up company. My last visit included going to the headquarters of WeWork labs, where collaborative workspaces encourage innovation in connecting people.

We visit Independence Hall, which was the first home built in Tel Aviv by the city's first mayor, Dizengoff. This is a humble structure where Israel was hastily proclaimed a state on May 14, 1948.

I keep the best for last. We always end the trip with a visit to Hebron, hosted by Yigal Kutai. He is so inspirational, and he truly reinforces the pride, integrity, and character of Israel and its amazing people. On this final day of our tour, Yigal arranges for us to be picked up from my home in Jerusalem in a bulletproof and bazooka-proof Ford Excursion eight-seater van. A donor made this generous gift so that security risk would not be the reason preventing people from visiting Hebron in the West Bank.

We arrive at Kiryat Arba, a secured and gated community with twelve thousand people in residence. Yigal arranges to have a welcome sign for each individual, with their full name on the door of what he calls a "seven star" penthouse. I, and other Beverly Hills residents, purchased this condominium and gave it to the community.

The windows face the ancient terraced mountains and hundreds of acres of vineyards, looking like a beautiful painting. Since there is no hotel in Kiryat Arba, the goal was for the community to be able to host dignitaries and other important guests to enjoy the five-bedroom suite.

An array of teas, coffee, drinks, Medjool dates, and assorted nuts and freshly baked rugelach are on the coffee table. This is Israeli hospitality.

Yigal took on the responsibility of developing community services in this region. His ultimate goal is that the people who live in this area will find it safe, attractive and desirable to build a life there. The place he could raise funds for this venture was from Jewish communities outside of Israel. This is how I, and my family, met him.

Traveling to the region over the years and seeing its development was a feat of success. His focus was to get residents to have a normal life, which is why the development features an Olympic-sized swimming pool and a state-of-the-art community center, where he would invite politicians and other celebrities to lecture and entertain the residents, as Hebron is a little isolated and somewhat separated from other Israeli communities.

He shows each group I bring, a short documentary that explains the history of Israel and its recapture in the Six-Day War in 1967 from Jordan. He tells us a little about his background and how he and his wife and his three kids ended up in this region. Born in Yemen, Yigal and his family moved to Israel in 1948, and he served as an entertainer for troops in the Israeli army. At the age of twenty-two he moved to Los Angeles, getting an internship with Rodgers & Cowen PR firm. He enrolled into an English course at UCLA, taught by his now-wife, Shifra, who is originally from Louisville, Kentucky.

Feeling homesick and a tinge of guilt during the Yom Kippur war of 1973, he and Shifra decided to get married and live in the new community, established in 1967, one-quarter mile from the center of Hebron.

The IDF provides security for the Israeli community in the area, which is now in excess of 12,000 people, who act as a buffer, and are a major support for the army. Yigal succeeded in his mission to ensure people would not leave the area and move to more tranquil and peaceful environments like Jerusalem or Tel Aviv.

Next stop we visit the Hadassah hospital, which is now a museum. Up to 1929 this Jewish hospital treated both Arabs and Jews. That was until an Arab riot erupted, because of rumors that the Jews were planning to seize control of the Temple Mount in Jerusalem. The event left sixty-nine Jews dead, seriously wounded, and maimed. The majority were doctors and nurses. Soon after, all the Hebron Jews were evacuated, never to return until Israel's recapture of the area in 1967.

After touring the museum with my last group in November, a watershed moment occurred that truly impacted me. As all five of us dispersed, looking at different parts of the still partially destroyed hospital museum, I was at the gift shop of the museum, where I was planning to buy ten bottles of Hebron's rich and bold Cabernet Sauvignon. I was getting the total of the bill, when one of my guests, Vince Calcagno—a Roman Catholic and a member of my CEO group—interjected and told the cashier, "No, don't take his card."

I insisted, "No way, Vince, am I going to let you pay for the wine I am buying for my home in Jerusalem."

Vince responded, "Efrem, you've done so much for me on this trip and for all of us. Do you realize what this experience means to me? You've touched my life. I am so thankful for your kindness, sharing your home, your friends. It's the least I can do."

His eyes began to tear up. I was so moved by Vince's experience of sincere appreciation that I also choked up and replied, "I'm so glad you are here and that you enjoyed this trip so much, but I'm not going to let you buy all this wine for my home." As I gave the perplexed cashier the money, I hugged Vince and thanked him again for his friendship.

While in Hebron, we stopped for an afternoon lunch in a condo I helped purchase, overlooking the Hebron Mountain. My purpose for buying this four-bedroom condo is to provide a weekly respite for the soldiers posted in the Hebron area, from the grueling tension in this military hot zone. Every week, for two hours, a platoon of twenty soldiers arrive and enjoy a sumptuous barbecue while being spiritually inspired and enlightened by Yigal's wisdom. I am always so grateful to the soldiers, and each of them has expressed profound gratitude for the introduction to Yigal.

IN CLOSING: LESSONS FOR A LUXE LIFE

It's good timing for me to complete the arduous, but rewarding, task of writing this book. I now have a clear mind to prepare for the multimillion-dollar facelift of the Luxe Rodeo Drive Hotel, scheduled to begin in the last quarter of 2019 and be completed by spring 2020. After all, the Luxe Rodeo Drive Hotel is on the world's foremost fashion street and it is the flagship of the Luxe chain. The goal of the upgrade is for our guests to experience well-appointed, relaxing rooms with thoughtfully convenient bathrooms. In addition to the attractive physical structure of the hotel, a big value we provide is the genuinely warm and caring spirit of every one of our team members, welcoming our guests back home.

I am happy that I have laid this foundation for a hotel empire. My team and I have established a luxury boutique brand of hotels which has the capacity to provide each guest a memorable experience, each employee the opportunity to build a successful hospitality career, and each community a valuable asset in their backyard. This is exactly what I want our brand of hotels to offer.

I purchased the Rodeo Drive hotel with the intent to replicate the hospitality concept in similar locations worldwide. I want to do this in

Boston on Commonwealth Avenue, on Michigan Avenue in Chicago, on Ocean Avenue in Miami, on Madison or Park Avenue in New York City, on Bond Street in London, and on Champs-Elysées or the Place Vendôme in Paris. In addition to Beverly Hills, Brentwood, and Los Angeles, we are already in the heart of Rome with the debut of the Luxe Rose Garden Hotel. We want to be at the center of it all; a Luxe branded hotel in every major city.

My team's talent is the ability to uncover hotel opportunities, polish them up, and communicate their beauty and their special qualities. That is really what we do best. We have the ability to find the consumer and excite them about the unique experience staying at one of our hotels. My goal is to bring classic hotels out of the shadows, restore them to their original grandeur, and usher them into the twenty-first century.

I have always had dreams of accomplishing many great things in my life, since back in Binyamina, Israel, where I was born. I have come a long way since then. I decided at a young age that I wanted to constantly grow as a person. I knew instinctively I had much to accomplish. And so it happens—a little more every day. This is a marathon, after all; not a sprint. I am proud of the courage shown by me and my team to fill a void in the hospitality industry. Throughout history, courage is the rarest of all the positive traits that revolutionize and change industries.

On these pages I have been able to share my journey with you about how I came from the desert of Israel, to the rough and challenging terrain of Australia, and made it all the way to the fulfillment of a dream in Beverly Hills, California. As I illustrated in this book, the simple act of "showing up" has always yielded results for me, and it can work for you as well. We are all given opportunities in life, and often our first instinct is not to accept that invitation, or pick up that call, or attend an event. I am living proof that you should, despite your first instinct to say "no." Whatever you do, show up!

This is the Luxe Life: a disciplined and goal-oriented existence that is, at the same time, meaningful, challenging, and fulfilling. It is a life I have crafted for myself. Though the formula for achieving success can be simple, it requires dedication, commitment, and hard work. For all my successes in life and in the business world, I am truly humbled and grateful because I worked for everything I have.

Over the years, I've discovered that genuinely sharing myself with others didn't diminish my power or influence as I initially thought it might. In the same way when you use one candle to light another, the result is "more light." The original light is not diminished. I want to believe in my heart that I have impacted people's lives and inspired them to make the world a better place. I've learned many lessons in life, and I would like to pass on this final thought to you: If I can do it, you can do it, too.

ABOUT THE AUTHORS

Efrem Harkham is the owner of the Luxe Sunset Boulevard Hotel and the Luxe Rodeo Drive Hotel in Los Angeles, California. He also owns and operates the Luxe Hotels brand, which currently consists of four luxury properties in Brentwood, Beverly Hills, Los Angeles, and Rome. Harkham's Luxe Collection provides sales, marketing, and reservation services for over seventy affiliated hotels around the world. He is also a family partner of Harkham Wines and the Hark Angel Foundation. This is his first book. He lives in Beverly Hills, California.

Mark Bego is a *New York Times* bestselling author of sixty-five books on rock 'n' roll and show business. He has over twelve million books in print in a dozen languages. His books include biographies of Elton John, the Supremes, Billy Joel, Cher, and Aretha Franklin. In 2017, he shifted gears to become a celebrity chef when he published his all-star cookbook, *Eat Like a Rock Star*. He chronicled his life in his 2010 memoir *Paperback Writer*. He lives in Tucson, Arizona.